D0699288

Music, Value and the Passions

Music, Value and the Passions

AARON RIDLEY

Cornell University Press | Ithaca and London

Copyright © 1995 by Cornell University

All rights reserved. Except for brief quotations in a review, this book, or
parts thereof, must not be reproduced in any form without permission in
writing from the publisher. For information, address Cornell University
Press, Sage House, 512 East State Street, Ithaca, New York 14850.

First published 1995 by Cornell University Press.

Printed in the United States of America

⊛ The paper in this book meets the minimum requirements
of the American National Standard for Information Sciences—
Permanence of Paper for Printed Library Materials, ANSI Z39.48-1984.

Library of Congress Cataloging-in-Publication Data

Ridley, Aaron.
　　Music, value, and the passions / Aaron Ridley.
　　　　p.　cm.
　　Includes bibliographical references and index.
　　ISBN 0–8014–3035–6
　　　1. Music—Philosophy and aesthetics.　2. Emotions (Philosophy)
I. title.
ML3847.R53　1995
781′.—dc20　　　　　　　　　　　　　　　　　94-42018
　　　　　　　　　　　　　　　　　　　　　　　　MN

To my parents

Contents

Preface

Recent years have seen the publication of several good books on the philosophy of music; and the furrow I have attempted to plow here would have been more unyielding and lonely had I not had the benefit of reading them first. Peter Kivy's *The Corded Shell* (1980) has been immensely valuable to me. Among its many virtues is the truly estimable one of advancing strong, positive positions with which one can really come to grips—positions that have stimulated me to pursue alternative and, I hope, constructive lines of thought. This book would have been quite different had I not studied Kivy's first. Jerrold Levinson's writings have also influenced me: indeed, my seventh chapter owes much to his essay "Music and Negative Emotion"—now collected in his *Music, Art, and Metaphysics* (1990). And all sorts of other bits—indefinable bits—could be attributed to him too, through that familiar osmotic process which defies proper referencing or acknowledgment. The most obvious debt of all, though, I owe to Malcolm Budd's tour de force of destruction, *Music and the Emotions* (1985). Budd demolishes virtually every existing way of accounting for music's relation to the passions. Yet to describe his book as merely negative would be to misrepresent it. He offers no positive account of his own, but his criticism is so rich as to be a distinct and unignorable spur to invention. I have pursued the following inquiry with one and often both eyes on Budd's arguments, in the hope of producing something that will—inter alia—function as a reply to the challenge I read his book as posing.

But my good fortune has extended beyond having seminal things to read. I have also been lucky in the people who have helped me by reading the things I have written. I am immensely grateful to Malcolm Budd, Stephen Davies, Jerrold Levinson, Alex Neill, Lauren Oppenhein, Brian Ridley, Michael Tanner and an anonymous reader for Cornell University Press for their criticisms—often hugely detailed and inconvenient—of some or all of what follows. I know that the changes I have made in response to these criticisms will only rarely have produced perfect conviction in those who raised them. But I do hope that the changes are at least in the right direction; and I know that making them has rendered my argument a good deal clearer now than it was before. To two of the people just mentioned I owe further, copious thanks. Not only did Alex Neill read large amounts of my manuscript and show me how to make parts of it better; he also had a direct hand in much of what he found there. Without our frequent, and frequently sober, discussions, very little would have found its way onto paper in the first place. To Michael Tanner I am grateful for slightly different reasons. As my Ph.D. supervisor, he entered his share of objections to versions of the arguments that now appear here. But what I will carry away from our meetings above all is a sense of the honesty and integrity with which philosophy, and especially the philosophy of music, can be done. If little trace of this appears in what follows then the fault is certainly not his.

Versions of parts of Chapters 3 and 6 have appeared previously in the *Journal of Aesthetics and Art Criticism:* "Bleeding Chunks: Some Remarks about Musical Understanding" in vol. 52 (Summer 1994), and "Musical Sympathies: The Experience of Expressive Music" in vol. 53 (Winter 1995). I thank the editor for his permission to use them here. I would also like to thank Roger Haydon of Cornell University Press for the unfailingly sardonic quality of his editorial interventions: he has been a pleasure to work with.

Last, and in many ways most, my thanks to those without whom it would have been impossible to write a book of any kind: my parents, Brian and Sylvia Ridley; my sister, Melissa, and her husband, Anil; Ann Spencer; and David Gibbins. They have all been extraordinarily generous, and have given me their help and support in a bewildering variety of forms, from the most elusive kind of encouragement to the most tangible kind of accommodation. I am sure that the much vaunted travails of authorship can rarely have been made so pleasant. Indeed, so ardent has everyone been in their efforts to make the book-writing period more burdensome for themselves than for me, I probably ought to think up a sequel at once . . .

Southampton, England   A. R.

Music, Value and the Passions

Introduction

An intimate association with the passions has always been one of music's most noted qualities. Indeed, only its relation to mathematics can rival that association for either frequency or antiquity of note. And if one is primarily interested in how music has been experienced by listeners, and in how it has struck them, then there can be little doubt that the laurels would go to the passions. A properly Pythagorean fascination with proportion must surely be more suited to the study, after all, than to the concert hall, to an experience that is theoretical rather than immediate. While the music is playing, it is the power of sound to articulate, explore, arouse, evoke, relieve, give voice to, give form to the passions which is likely to be striking. When the experience is over, one may of course adopt a more reflective stance. Perhaps if one's concerns are geometric, or even mystical, one will give thought to the "music of the spheres," to the preponderance of certain ratios in music and in the world. But equally, if one is struck by the quality of the experience itself, one may reflect afterward on the strange and remarkable fact that music should bear any relation to the passions whatever, that sound should have so singular a power. For what could it be in a mere series of noises—blown, struck, plucked, sung, bowed—which has the power to put one in mind of, even in a state of, passion?

The Greeks attributed such power to the peculiar characters

of the various modes, linking each mode with some special kind of passion.[1] In the early eighteenth century, it was thought that the link between music and the passions was secured by the musical imitation of passionate voices.[2] A hundred and fifty years later, quasi-Darwinian explanations gained currency: our passionate responses to music were atavistic vestiges of a primal response to the mating cry.[3] Yet in the same century, and against what was then the trend, it was also being argued that the relation between music and the passions was so vague, or else so inexplicable, that we would do better to confine our attention to the purely musical aspects of the musical experience.[4] And it is this latter view which, with the rise of positivist techniques of analysis, has held sway ever since. A sophisticated and specialized terminology has been developed, and with it an array of procedures designed to lay bare the deep structure of musical processes and relations. Often penetrating, and sporting all the accoutrements of objectivity, analysis has become the only really respectable way to investigate and to talk about music. The exclusion of the passions from such talk, presumably on grounds of subjectivity and irrationality, has been all but complete; and efforts to reinclude them have, by and large, been rebuffed, and rebuffed with varying amounts of rudeness.

A recent monograph on music and the passions was dismissed outright by one reviewer, for example, not for its arguments but for its subject matter.[5] The passions were irrelevant to musical experience, he said; and anyone who, ignorantly, insisted on describing music in the language of the passions

1. See, for instance, Plato and Aristotle on musical education: *Republic* 3 and *The Politics*, 8.5.

2. See, e.g., *Works of Thomas Reid,* ed. William Hamilton (Edinburgh and London, 1895), 1:504.

3. See Edmund Gurney, *The Power of Sound* (London, 1880).

4. See, e.g., Eduard Hanslick, *On the Musically Beautiful,* trans. G. Payzant (Indianapolis: Hackett, 1986).

5. R. A. Sharpe, reviewing Peter Kivy's *The Corded Shell* (Princeton: Princeton University Press, 1980) in the *British Journal of Aesthetics* (1981): 81–82.

should be encouraged to learn the proper terminology instead. In his view, the whole subject merited no serious investigation. But clearly he was wrong. For even if it were true that the "proper" terminology was in some relevant way more illuminating than the terminology of the passions, the function and origin of the improper terminology would still be an interesting and legitimate subject of inquiry. But—and much more crucially—it is a very odd thing to claim that an aspect of musical experience that is, as a matter of fact, central to the musical appreciation of the vast majority of listeners is simply "irrelevant." At most, it will be irrelevant to the small number of people who are proficient in the language of analysis. To those who are interested in music as it is actually experienced, in how music has come to occupy a unique and distinctive place in our culture, the passionate aspects of musical listening will be not merely not irrelevant but central, and will constitute a self-evidently proper object of investigation. The analytic trend, in ignoring what had for so long been recognized as one of music's most powerful attributes, has done music and the study of music a disservice, however impressive its other achievements may have been. Music is the language of the passions; and any adequate conception of music must have something to say about its passionate connections.

In what follows, then, I will attempt to say something about them. I will attempt to relate those connections to the question of musical value. My own experience strongly suggests that of the value which I attach to certain pieces of music, much is predicated upon the passionate aspects of what I hear and of what I experience when I hear them; and I know, in an informal, empirical way, that I am not unusual in this. Thus I want to suggest that any comprehensive exploration of the value we attach to music must take notice of the passions with which music may be associated, and that any account of music's passionate connections must also, and by the same token, contribute to a deeper understanding of musical value. This is not of course to say that its passionate connections are the sole or the most important features of music to which we attach value, or even that all valuable music has any such connections. It is merely to say that value and the passions are often found together in the experience of music, and that an attempt to draw any conclusions about one of them will almost certainly entail conclusions about the other. I will concentrate here on music and the passions; but I will try to indicate at appropriate points along the way what part in a wider investigation into musical value my account might play; and I will try, where appropriate, to make that part explicit. My efforts in this direction should thus, if they are found convincing, add richness and also plausibility to the principal claims I mean to make.

Before going any further, though, I think it might be as well to lay some cards on the table. I have spoken of "music" so far as if it were a simple, unitary phenomenon. Yet of course there are many varieties of music. No doubt the kind of investigation I am undertaking could, in different hands, have concentrated on popular music, say, or jazz, or on the music of some far Eastern isle. But my own passion happens to be for Western art music of the last three centuries—from, roughly, Monteverdi to, roughly, Tippett; and it is on this kind of music that I will be focusing. I hope that what I have to say about such music will have application to other kinds of music; indeed, I am sure that it will have. But the first test of my case must be whether it is adequate to the experience of Western art music. It is from this tradition that I have drawn my examples, and it is my own experience of this tradition that has given me anything to say about music at all.

I have tried to select my examples from the mainstream, avoiding reference to obscure or esoteric repertoire; but I have been obliged, inevitably, to assume that anyone reading this book has an experience of music, and an engagement with it, that is similar to my own. And this doesn't, in the end, seem to me to be a liability. As a listener I have immoderate enthusiasms. But these enthusiasms do tend to be for things like

Beethoven symphonies rather than, say, the organ works of Matthias Weckmann or the chamber music of Raff. So in a fairly clear sense my tastes are conventional ones; and the kind of listener I have in mind when I refer simply to "the listener" is a fairly conventional listener, rather like me. Such a listener goes to concerts, buys or borrows recordings, listens to them even when there are no domestic chores to be done at the same time, reads the odd book about music, likes to talk about music, plays an instrument, perhaps, and is perfectly convinced that a life without music would be hardly a life at all. Such listeners will of course have preferences, and many of those will be different from mine—which means that the odd disagreement is sure to arise over my choice of examples, especially when those examples involve value judgments. But because the account that I am trying to develop here is intended to include reference to musical value, such examples can hardly be avoided. Suffice it to say that none of my arguments *depends* upon the specific value judgments I make. Other judgments on other examples might have served as well. But without some such set of examples and their accompanying judgments, I am sure that my case would have been made pointlessly weaker by underillustration. Should my presumed reader (the ordinary, amateur devotee of Western art music) wish to be nicer about, say, Richard Strauss than I am, then that's fine; but there is nothing in such a disagreement which need interfere with that reader's assessment of my efforts to relate music, and the value we place on it, to the passions. The value judgments I make illustrate my argument: they do not underpin it.

Let me conclude these introductory remarks with a brief indication of how the following chapters are organized. In Chapters 1 and 2 I assemble some of the materials, distinctions and strategies I think are essential; in the next four chapters I develop the main body of the account; in Chapter 7 I address one serious objection to it; and in the last chapter I extend and refine the account as far as I am able to. A theoretical minefield, however, lies between music and the passions; and I very much doubt that the route through it which I have tried to plot here will be found unobjectionable. But I do hope that it will at least be thought worth objecting to. For what I have written constitutes a defense of the common-sense position on music—that music is indeed significantly and valuably related to the passions—against the contemporary orthodoxies of musicological analysis. And if I have succeeded in leaving the ball in the analysts' court, then my argument will have done most of what I wanted it to do.

CHAPTER ONE

Music and the Passions

If you ask me tomorrow or any other day why some sounds
are sad and others glad I shall not be able to tell you. Not
even your Papa could tell you that. Why, what a thing to ask,
my pets! If you knew that, you would know everything. Good
night, my dears, good night.

    —Rebecca West, *The Fountain Overflows*

There are an enormous number of ways in which an object can
be related to the passions, or in which it can be referred to by
using terminology drawn from the language of the passions.
Some of these ways will be more interesting than others, and at
the outset it will rarely be obvious which ways are which. It
certainly isn't obvious when the objects in question are pieces of
music. It is for this reason that I have chosen the word *passion*
as a generic term, intended to range impartially over a number of conceptually distinct phenomena—emotions, moods,
feelings—without according theoretical primacy to any of them.
In due course it will be necessary to distinguish quite sharply
within this range. But the generic term allows us for the moment to go about our business without getting bogged down in
a series of needless presuppositions. Were we to declare in advance, for instance, that what is of prime aesthetic importance is
the musical *expression* of *emotion*—specifically—we would at
once rule out much that might prove in time to play a part in a
full or successful account of the relation between music and the
passions, and we might impede even the completion of the
narrower project embarked upon. Malcolm Budd concludes his
recent survey of the principal philosophical accounts of this

relation with the following remark: "If my arguments are correct, a new theory of music is needed; and if that theory is to be
revealing it will, I believe, have to be less monolithic than the
theories I have rejected."[1] One preemptive gesture toward heterogeneity, then, will be to begin with a catholic conception
of the passions with which music may be associated, and with
an open mind as to which *mode* of association is the most
germane.

I

A survey of the various types of relation between music and
passions, then, is clearly the place to start. We can and do make a
great variety of statements about music that have reference to
the passions, and we will find it useful later to have them classed
into groups. From among our remarks about music, it is perhaps most convenient to begin with the type that seems widest
in scope, as when we claim that a certain piece of music is
"moving." It is worth noticing, however, that when we speak of
a piece of music as "moving" we do not always mean that we, as
listeners, are moved to some particular passion (our state may
be inchoate) or even necessarily that what we are moved to is a
passion at all. So when, for example, I say that the thought of
someone improvident has moved me to lecture him, I mean in
the first place that I have been moved by the thought of him to
an *action* of a certain kind; and it may be that this is all I mean.
For it does not seem that in order to be moved to lecture
someone I must first or also be moved to some passion with
regard to him, or with regard to myself in my role as lecturer to
the improvident. I need be neither contemptuous nor pitying
nor ashamed of him; nor proud, enamored or full of myself—
however much I might seem to be those things from the outside. I may, in terms of passion, be quite indifferent. At the

1. Malcolm Budd, *Music and the Emotions* (London: Routledge and Kegan
Paul, 1985), p. 176.

minimum it seems that in order to be moved in this way I need merely hold a certain set of beliefs (for example, that the person I lecture is improvident, and that I know better than he what he should do) and perhaps have certain desires (such as the desire to help him, or the desire, in general, to pontificate); and, as will become apparent in a while, beliefs and desires are neither separately nor jointly sufficient conditions of passion. So when we say that a piece of music moves us we need not necessarily mean that it moves us to a passion: we might be moved by the music to have a go at composing something similar ourselves. Insofar as to be moved is to be moved to action in the absence of passion, then, the phenomenon does not directly concern us.

But more usually, to be moved *is* to be moved to some affective state, to some passion. We very often elaborate upon our claim to be moved—saying, for example, that nothing cheers us up like a good dose of Haydn, or irritates us like Respighi. In remarks of this kind, we make clear reference to a particular passion (cheerfulness or irritation), and we clearly hold the music responsible, in some sense, for moving us to it. But it should be noticed that the range of possible passions to which music may move us is not uniform; and in particular that the sense in which music is responsible for our being moved does not remain constant across that range. For a piece of music may be related in a variety of ways to the passions which we experience, such that the part that it takes in our coming to feel as we do will be different in each. It is therefore insufficient to say merely that the music "makes" us experience certain passions.

Consider the possible range of passion that I might experience in relation to someone's face, that may be occasioned by my perception of that person's face. To begin with, the face may be familiar to me, and to perceive it nearby may hearten or distress me. Or I may find it a nice or a pretty face, and be enraptured by it; or a huge and impressive face, and feel awed. If the face is injured or scarred, its imperfections may strike me with melancholy; and if, in virtue of the exceptional mobility or unorthodox disposition of its parts, it seems to me a strange and amazing face, then perhaps I will become hysterical or bemused. It is important to note that in each of these examples it is by some aspect of the face itself that I am moved—by its sheer dimensions to awe, for instance, or by its beauty to rapture— and that in none of these cases is what moves me a fact about the *expressiveness* or the *expression* of the face, or the relation in which the face stands to any passion but my own. Thus, it may be by virtue simply of its unprecedented arrangement that a face amuses me, quite irrespective of what connection a face so arranged may be supposed to bear to the affective state of its owner. I shall call cases of this kind, where I am moved to passion by aspects of a thing that are neither expressive nor related to passions other than my own, *cognitive responses.*

It is clear that music may be the occasion of cognitive response. For example: I may turn on the radio, hear Strauss's *Alpine Symphony* going on, and become distressed; or I may be enraptured by the sensuous beauty of *La Mer.* The complexity of a Bach fugue, the duration of a Bruckner symphony, or the volume of a huge orchestral tutti—any of them may render me awed. It is conceivable that the incompleteness of Schubert's Eighth might sadden me, or that Britten's arrangements of folk songs infuriate; but the sheer energy and speed of much Prokofiev, or the eccentric inventiveness of Haydn, is bound to leave me excited, enlivened and cheerful. Clearly any list of this kind cannot hope to exhaust the phenomena. But such a list ought at least to give an idea of the diversity of cognitive response which music may elicit, and an indication of how various are the aspects of music (its sensuousness, complexity, completeness, rapidity and so on) to which we may thus respond. Roughly, these aspects can be categorized as follows: there are qualitative aspects—for example, of the work as a whole, the value that the listener detects in it; of its melodies, harmonies and rhythms, how beautiful they are; of its timbres and textures, how sensuous. There are quantitative aspects—for example, the speed, duration or volume of a work. And there are technical aspects—such as a work's structure or organization, the relations it comprises, or its tonal complexity: those features, in other words, which may be approached through musical analysis. Now it is clear that these divisions are not nearly so sharp as such categorizations might suggest. The *alla danza tedesca* movement of Beethoven's Quartet in B♭, Op. 130, for example, may strike me as beautiful and swift and complex; but my cognitive response to it—of enlivened admiration, say— is not distributed accordingly, but is rather a unitary response to its beautifully swift complexity, or to its swiftly complex beauty, or whatever. So by the threefold division proposed no more than a convenient device is intended; in particular, it should not be thought that in one and the same response we may not react to aspects belonging to two, or to all three, of the suggested categories. And finally we should note that in one further aspect—that as created object—the music may elicit from us cognitive responses, this time to the manner of creation achieved *within* any or all of these categories; so that occasionally we admire the effort and struggle with which a certain degree of technical complexity has audibly been bought, for example (as in the *Grosse Fuge*), whereas at other times we admire the facility with which a beautiful melody sounds as though it had been tossed off (as in almost any Schubert).

I turn now to a second form of passionate response that music can occasion, which I shall call *sympathetic response*. A sympathetic response is one elicited from a person in virtue of the expressive features of an object perceived—features that, however, the person does *not* think of as standing in significant relation to anyone else's passions (or to none but those of persons similarly placed *vis-à-vis* the object). So that when, for example, I am made melancholy by the sight of a weeping willow, I do not suppose the willow to experience any passion, and (unless I know or believe it to have been planted for such reasons) neither do I suppose it to be the outward manifestation of someone else's passion. Rather, I recognize in the willow features reminiscent of melancholy expressions (its trailing, drooping qualities) and respond to them by becoming melancholy myself. The willow puts me in mind of melancholy, in which mind I am saddened. Now I might equally, having been put in mind of melancholy, respond not by becoming melancholy myself, but with impatience or distaste, depending upon my temper and disposition. Responses of this kind are also sympathetic responses; for in becoming annoyed by the willow's expressive features, by its melancholy droop, I still do not conceive it as standing in significant relation to the passion of another. So sympathetic responses may be of either consonant or contrasting character with the expressive features that occasion them. Faces can occasion responses in both of these ways. I may respond gloomily to the habitually gloomy countenance of a friend, knowing full well that this particular expression of hers has no probable connection with her real state. Or her looking like that might exasperate me.

Now it should be clear from this that music can elicit sympathetic response. For in virtue of certain of its features music seems able to recall to us, or to put us in mind of, particular passions to which we may respond—so that I may be made chirpy by the chirpiness of a Rossini string sonata, or sullen by the high spirits of a madrigal, without in either case relating expressive jollity to anyone's passion but my own. For I do not suppose the music to experience passion, and nor do I (need I) suppose it to be the outward sign of anybody else's passion, for example the composer's. Rather, I recognize in the music features reminiscent of or related to certain expressions, to which I then respond. Where my response *may* have reference to someone else, of course—though not to his passion—is when I respond, perhaps admiringly, to the composer's ability so to order these features of his music. And according to the definition I have offered, this too will count as a sympathetic response.

But more usually, of course, when we respond to the expressive features of someone's face, for example, we do conceive of those features as standing in significant relation to someone's passion other than our own; so that what we respond to is the passion to which we understand the other as giving facial expression. This kind of response I shall call *empathetic response;* and it too may be consonant or contrasting in character. To a friend's expression of distress I might respond by feeling *with* her, by becoming myself distressed. Or I may have contrasting responses, such as pity or *schadenfreude.* In either case, I take her expression (which might consist in a spree of willow planting) to signal something about the state in which she finds herself, and in each case it is to her in this state that I empathetically respond.

Now we speak as if music were sometimes the occasion of empathetic response. It may seem to me when I listen to the finale of Tchaikovsky's Sixth Symphony that the terminal depression of which its expressive features put me in mind is Tchaikovsky's own depression; and it may be for the depressed Tchaikovsky that my empathetic response is felt (perhaps of depression, perhaps of pity). Or alternatively, the passion to which I conceive of these expressive features as significantly related may be not the composer's but that of a friend, whose compulsive and relentless listening to the symphony I understand as an expression of her own depressed condition; and I may feel with her, or for her. In each case I take the expressive features of the work to be expressions of *somebody's* passion, and it is to the person in that state that I empathetically respond. It should be noted briefly how complex this kind of response can be: it might happen, for example, that I say that I am cheered upon hearing a *Liebeslieder* waltz to learn that Brahms could be jolly (as I might be to come across my serious and depressive friend dancing a jig), without finding that the instance of jollity thus expressed (by waltz or by jig) is itself of a kind that I can empathetically respond to. I may merely be cheered to find that jollity, as a passion, is one possible for

Brahms (or my friend) to have, while remaining indifferent to him when he is actually in it. And there are other varieties of empathetic response. I may admire the composer for his capacity to experience the passions of which his music puts me in mind—just as, in the context of sympathetic response, I admire his capacity to compose music having features that so put me in mind (and, indeed, as I admire him in virtue of those other aspects of his music to which I respond cognitively). And so on. The range and scope of such responses is very wide and varied. But this brief sketch should have indicated sufficiently some of the principal forms they may take; and to a number of these we shall return in some detail later.

One final variety of response should be mentioned, however, which I shall call *associative response*. I respond to music associatively when it elicits the passion in me that it does solely in virtue of the association that the music has, for me, with something else, which would by itself elicit that response. So that when I gnash my teeth at a piece which reminds me of some irksome period of my life, or when I treat minimalist music with contempt because I find the sort of person who mostly enjoys minimalist music contemptible, I respond associatively. In the first case, my teeth are gnashed at the thought of the unhappy time that I had—and would have been gnashed at the thought of it whatever had brought it to mind. And in the second case, my contempt is for the sort of person who likes minimalist music, against whom, for the purposes of this example, I must be supposed to hold something quite apart from this specific predilection. In neither case is there anything intrinsic to the music itself that grounds my response: if another work had featured large during my more noisome moments, then it would have been at that work that I subsequently gnashed my teeth; and if the kind of person who likes minimalist music had instead conceived a passion for Vivaldi, then I would hold Vivaldi in contempt. But I shall return briefly to associative responses in the next chapter.

For now, let us review some of the principal senses that the claim to be cheered up by a piece of music can have. First, we may respond cognitively to the music: we may be cheered by qualitative, quantitative or technical aspects of it (or of its performance)—aspects that are thought of in relation not to the music's expressive features (if any), or to any passion but our own. Second, we may experience sympathetic response to the music: we may be cheered by the exuberance, say—or, if we are so disposed, by the sadness—of which certain expressive features in the music (or of its performance) have put us in mind, without supposing such exuberant or sad features to bear any relation to the passions of another. Third, the music may occasion empathetic response in us: we may be cheered by another person's exuberance (perhaps the composer's, perhaps the performer's)—or, if we are so given, feel cheered by another's sadness—of which we take certain expressive features in the music (which put us in mind of exuberance or sadness) to be the outward manifestation. Fourth, and running alongside these first three, we may be cheered because of what we conceive someone to have *done* (perhaps the composer, perhaps the performer): we may admire the handling, in composition or performance, of certain of the music's qualitative, quantitative or technical aspects; we may admire the deployment, in composition or performance, of certain of the music's expressive features; and we may admire the composer or performer for the capacity to experience the passions of which we take the music's expressive features to be the outward manifestation. Fifth, and finally, we may respond associatively to the music: we may be cheered because the music reminds us of a cheerful period of our lives. So it is clear that there are many senses in which music may be the occasion of our being moved to particular passions; and that when we say a work "makes" us feel such-and-such, we may intend any of these senses to be understood (or indeed all of them, or several in combination: for it is plain that none precludes any other); and we should notice in addition that ordinary usage may be vaguer even than this, having it merely that a work *is* such-and-such, when one or more of the foregoing senses is intended.

II

The passions to which music moves us are not the only passions to which music can be related, however; or—perhaps more accurately—our talk of passionate response to music does not exhaust the class of possible statements about music which make use of affective terminology. And we have already seen the truth of this remark in the preceding section. For our sympathetic and empathetic responses *depend* upon musical characteristics which are to be picked out by means of affective terminology; upon the expressive features of music, in other words. So that when we say that Tchaikovsky's Sixth Symphony puts us in mind of terminal depression, we already, whether we are moved or not, detect in the work qualities that we describe in the language of passion—qualities expressive of terminal depression.

There would appear to be two ways in which music can be related to passion in this sense—by conventional expressiveness, and by creative expressiveness. Conventional expressiveness is what much film music, and most popular music, largely consists of, though of course it is not restricted to these genres. It occurs whenever stock expressive devices are employed—such as sweeping string tunes to suggest love, or slow saxophonic riffs to suggest melancholy. Sometimes these devices acquire their conventional roles by what amounts to stipulation, so that much of the stern, doom-laden quality of the *Dies Irae* chant derives from association with its text, and much of the martial exhilaration of brass band music is derived from its use by the army. And sometimes these devices acquire their conventional roles through simple overuse, so that what was once, in its earlier history, an original expressive feature, becomes later on something more like a signifier—as a certain kind of atonal doodling has become in many horror and suspense movies. A piece of music is conventionally expressive to the extent that it restricts itself to the use of such devices. But because some minimal inventiveness is required to use even these (i.e., you've got to come up with something that *counts* as a sweeping string tune), the expressiveness of a work is rarely if ever exclusively conventional.

Creative expressiveness, by contrast, is expressiveness that relies for its effect upon more than mere stock devices. Such expressiveness may occur when a composer exploits some already available musical item to novel expressive effect. For example, the yearning of the prelude to *Tristan* appears to owe almost nothing to convention, even though the features responsible for that expressive effect—the various suspensions, and of course the "Tristan chord" itself—had been used before, for instance by Chopin. Wagner took those features and combined them in such a way as to reveal in the combination an altogether unprecedented expressive potential. By 1905, however, when Josef Suk employed much the same features in the finale of his *Asrael* Symphony, the novelty of the expressive effect had largely worn off, and the resultant expressiveness sounds fairly conventional. Another way in which a piece of music can be creatively expressive is by its composer simply *inventing* the means by which an expressive effect is achieved. An example here might be the unique sound world invented by the later Mahler, out of which the extraordinary expressive effects of, for instance, *Das Lied von der Erde* are conjured. A work is creatively expressive, then, to the extent that it avoids relying on stock devices. But because all (or most) music is composed against the background of a common musical culture and exhibits in varying degrees its indebtedness thereto, the expressiveness of a work is rarely if ever exclusively creative. Conventional and creative expressiveness are the means by which music (or performances of it—for conventionally and creatively expressive measures are plainly available to executants also) may be significantly related to passions that are not ascribed to anybody (or to anything).[2] They are what we respond to in music when we experience sympathetic response.

But as we saw in the previous section, music may seem to elicit from us empathetic responses also. In these cases, we *do* ascribe the passions of which the music is expressive to someone: to the composer, perhaps, or the performer, or—if the music is opera—to the character whom the performer represents. And we may make these ascriptions whether or not we are moved. So music may be taken to stand in significant relation not only to passions in a general sense but also to particular episodes of passion. This latter relation depends upon the former. For it is only by identifying the passions which music is (conventionally or creatively) expressive of, and then by interpreting them as *someone's,* that such a relation can be established.

There is, however, scope for much ambiguity here. For just as the phrase "the music makes us cheerful" has many senses, so it is not always clear what is meant by the statement "the music expresses depression"—it is uncertain, that is, whether the depression referred to is to be thought of as *someone's* depression. In an attempt to avoid confusion, then, I shall adopt in what is to come the following distinction: when the music is to be understood as standing in significant relation to passions in a general sense, that is, to passions that are ascribed to nobody, I shall say that the music is *expressive of* those passions; and when those passions *are* to be attributed to somebody, that is, when the music is to be understood as standing in relation to specific episodes of passion, I shall say that the music *expresses* those passions, or that it is an *expression of* them. It should by these means be possible to remain clear about what is meant at any juncture: weeping willows by themselves are *expressive of*

2. In what follows, I shall understand by *expressiveness* a combination of the conventional and the creative, except where explicitly stated.

melancholy; but planted by my grieving friend they *express* melancholy—hers.

We are now in a position to appreciate how many different things a statement like "Chopin's Funeral March is sad" can mean. It can mean any of the senses of "makes us" sad detailed at the end of Section I, it can mean "is expressive of" sadness, or it can mean "expresses" sadness, as we have just seen. It can also mean a combination of almost any of these. In Section IV I shall attempt to determine what problems, from a philosophical point of view, attend these various senses in which music can be related to passion. But first we need to ask: what exactly *is* a passion?

III

I said at the beginning that I was using the term *passion* in a generic way to cover a range of distinct phenomena. It is now time to start distinguishing more closely. For instance, I wish to mark off *sensations* from passions. Sensations are not intentional states, nor are they dispositions to experience intentional states. When I experience pain or pins and needles, I do not feel, nor am I disposed to feel, pain or pins and needles *about* anything; therefore, insofar as intentionality, or disposition to intentionality, is a criterion of the mental, sensations seem not to be mental states.[3] Further, a sensation is something that happens to you. When I push a knife into my foot, the sensation "pain" happens to me; when blood begins to circulate again around my arm after it's been wedged beneath the pillow all night, the sensation "pins and needles" happens to me. In both cases the sensation has a position in space (my foot, or my arm), and a cause (the incision, or the return of blood). Therefore, inasmuch as position in space and etiology are criteria of the physical, sensations appear to be physical events. It follows from

3. As Alan Tormey has pointed out in his *The Concept of Expression* (Princeton: Princeton University Press, 1971), p. 10.

this that sensations are susceptible of physiological, causal explanation rather than conceptual analysis; and also that, insofar as passions are mental states, sensations are not to be conceived by themselves as passions (although they may be *involved* in passion). Therefore, if any of the phenomena I have detailed in Sections I and II are sensations *simpliciter,* their explanation will be a matter for physiology rather than philosophy. But a swift review of those phenomena should show that none of them reduces without remainder to sensation as I have here characterized it. So if sensations are distinct from passions, what are we to say about passions? I have suggested that they are (at least in part) mental phenomena and that intentionality, or disposition to intentionality, is a criterion of the mental. Passions, therefore, must consist (at least in part) of intentional states, or of dispositions toward intentional states. We shall see in the next section how the latter alternative is sometimes realized; but let us first examine those passions which are predominantly intentional states.

According to one influential account, *emotions* are such states. Emotions are construed as involving thoughts or beliefs about objects, persons or states of affairs. This construction derives from Aristotle,[4] and it has since received a number of different formulations. Few of these, however, can match the clarity or precision of that which appears as the first chapter of Malcolm Budd's *Music and the Emotions.* Budd suggests that his account should be understood as only a model, "to which many emotions conform but from which other emotions or other states of mind diverge in various ways and to different degrees"; for "the emotions . . . form a heterogeneous class, and one, moreover, of which the membership is uncertain." We ought not therefore "attempt to capture the essence of an emotion in a definition of the form 'Each emotion is . . . ,' " unless we wish to be besieged by a tiresome and ultimately futile string of coun-

---

4. Aristotle, *Rhetoric,* 1378–88.

terexamples.[5] For sufficiently many emotions *do* conform to the model, even if it might require supplementation in some cases. We should note here that, despite these caveats, it is nonetheless necessary that the model should capture something that is essential to emotion *in general,* even if not to every single type of emotion. Otherwise the model is a model not of emotion but, at best, of some different kind of mental state; or perhaps it will model nothing. So Budd's account must, if it is to be useful, consist in a definition of the form "Mostly/standardly/in general, emotions are (*at least*) . . . ," even if nothing truly exhaustive is possible. And it seems that his account may indeed be understood in this way.

The style of definition Budd favors is the following: an emotion is "a thought experienced with pain or pleasure." Fear, then, for example, "is distress at the thought of danger to oneself or someone or something one cares about"; "remorse is distress at the thought that one has acted wrongly"; hope is pleasure at the thought of some possible future state; and so on. This style of definition has the following significant characteristics: each emotion involves a particular kind of thought, so that the concept of a particular thought is part of the concept of the emotion, and so that "someone experiences one of these emotions only if he is of a certain opinion, or views things in a certain way, . . . or a certain thought occurs to him"; each emotion involves a reaction to this thought, which is either positive or negative: "a form of satisfaction or dissatisfaction, pleasure or pain, . . . delight or distress," so that the "hedonic tone" of an emotion is "dictated by the concept of the emotion";[6] and, although each emotion involves a particular kind of thought, different emotions can involve exactly the same thought, so that "it is because pity and *schadenfreude* involve different reactions to the same thought—the one reaction is

5. Budd, *Music and the Emotions,* p. 14.
6. Ibid., pp. 4–5, 129.

distress, the other is pleasure—that they are different emotions." Therefore the emotions are "the various forms in which kinds of thought can be experienced with kinds of pleasure or pain."[7]

Now emotions may involve more than thoughts experienced with pleasure or pain; and Budd concedes that among these other elements may be some that are essential to the characterization of certain emotions. An especially intimate conceptual connection with such elements, then, is one of the means by which an emotion may "diverge in various ways and to different degrees" from the model. But Budd considers neither of the two additional elements with which he deals to be so basic to emotion *in general* as are thoughts and hedonic tones. He rejects desire; for while desire may be intrinsic to certain emotions—as the desire to escape may be intrinsic to fear—it can be argued that desire is a phenomenon logically secondary to hedonic tone: "Someone does not desire something if he does not view its prospect with pleasure or the likelihood of its not coming to pass with displeasure." So desire is less basic to emotion than is hedonic tone; and in any case, "the introduction of an aspect of desire into the emotions would not always be justified. For some emotions lack desires as constituents." He rejects "bodily feelings" likewise (what I have called *sensations*): for although someone experiencing emotion often experiences bodily feelings, "it is not part of the nature of any emotion that someone experiences that emotion only if he experiences a particular set of bodily feelings"; indeed, "it is not a conceptual truth that two creatures, each of whom experiences the same emotion and feels changes in his body, must feel the same processes take place in their bodies. . . . Consequently, no matter how close the links between emotions and bodily feelings may be in our lives, it is unnecessary to introduce a reference to particular sets of bodily feelings into the definitions of the emotions, but, at most, in the case of some emotions, a reference to the occurrence of unspecified bodily feelings."[8] So al-

7. Ibid., p. 5.
8. Ibid., pp. 8–10.

though desires and sensations may be intrinsic to certain emotions, neither is profitably to be imported into the definition of emotion in general. The definition of emotion, then, of which Budd's model consists, may be given thus: "Mostly/ standardly/in general, emotions are (at least) thoughts experienced with pain or pleasure; some emotions also involve desires and/or sensations." To complete the picture, however, we should take note of one further observation. Budd does not claim that whenever we experience emotion we have in mind some clearly formulated abstract thought, to which we then react. Rather, he says, the thought "will be conveyed or embodied in an experience—a perceptual experience, an experiential form of memory or an exercise of the imagination—and the progress of the emotion will be governed by the manner in which the experience develops."[9]

Though I believe Budd's model to be substantially correct, it seems to me to be too simple. In particular, I do not think he gives sufficient weight to the experiential character of emotion, whether that character be sought in sensation or elsewhere. I can bring this point out best by detailing two contrasting reservations I have about the role that Budd assigns to hedonic tone—hedonic tone being the nearest to an *experiential* feature that he allows into his definition. The first reservation concerns the *necessity* of hedonic tone, as characterized, to emotion. For it seems neither that every emotion is necessarily pleasant or unpleasant to experience (i.e., that every emotion *has* a hedonic tone) nor that every emotion which does have a hedonic tone is necessarily always pleasant or unpleasant to experience (i.e., that hedonic tone is "dictated by the concept of the emotion"). Budd characterizes envy as follows: "Envy is pain at the thought of an advantage enjoyed by another."[10] But it is not clear that envy is in fact necessarily painful. For the experience of envy *need* not be the resentful experience that Budd describes. It can be true of one that one envies someone, without it being true

9. Ibid., p. 13.
10. Ibid., p. 4.

that one wishes no longer to envy that person, which one would have to wish if one truly found *painful* the thought of an advantage enjoyed by another. So envy can be either without hedonic tone *or* painful. Therefore the hedonic tone of envy is not "dictated by the concept of the emotion." Now, it could be that this shows no more than that envy is one of the emotions which diverges in various ways from the model—albeit, here, in a rather significant way; or it is possible that envy is not properly to be understood as an emotion, although that would be surprising. What may be indicated, however, is that the model's strong commitment to positive or negative hedonic tone either is too strong or else is misplaced; and that the attempt to define an emotion requires some reference to what the emotion is actually *like* to experience.

Any such suspicion is strengthened by my second reservation, which concerns the *characterization* of hedonic tone. Throughout his discussion, Budd is careful to modulate the nature of hedonic tone imputed according to the nature of emotion discussed; and as we have seen, he speaks of "*kinds* of pleasure or pain" (my italics). So the tone of emotion is not merely positive or negative: we have "pleasure" and "pain," "distress," "discomfort" and "comfort," "satisfaction" and "dissatisfaction," each term applied, where it appears, appropriately to a particular emotion. Now it is well that this should be so. For in certain cases the substitution of other hedonic tone words will distort, or miss, the character of the emotion in question. "Acute distress at the thought of the death of someone who is dear to one" is a formulation to which grief will conform. But "acute dissatisfaction at the thought of the death of someone who is dear to one" is not. No doubt there is some murky state of mind thus to be captured; but it is not grief. And nor is grief an exception in this context. Consider joy described in terms of extreme comfort, or love in terms of satisfaction (or even of pleasure). So it seems that emotions involve different forms of hedonic tone (different "kinds of pleasure and pain") and that these tones differ not simply with respect to their positive or negative characters. This might mean either that there are subclasses of emotion, for example the distressful emotions, or the comfortable ones, such that an emotion is misrepresented when it is assigned to the wrong subclass, as grief is misrepresented when construed as "dissatisfying"; or it might mean that certain emotions have hedonic tones of still greater specificity, such that those tones may be characterized only by reference to the emotions involving them. The first possibility seems plainly to be true, as the foregoing discussion establishes. But if the second should also be true then the consequences for Budd's model are significant. For if certain emotions involve hedonic tones specific to them then they cannot be defined in terms of those tones (except by ostension); and any model of emotion including such a definition is incomplete or circular to the extent that it depends upon it.

Consider remorse. Remorse can plausibly be construed as a member of the subclass of distressful emotions, and can be characterized as "distress at the thought of having acted wrongly." But this formulation does not uniquely designate remorse—one may merely be afraid of getting caught. It is possible to circumvent this by expanding the thought that is experienced with distress so that fear of apprehension is ruled out. But there are still further potential designates from among the distressful emotions: one might be disappointed or infuriated with oneself, or ashamed, or afraid that one might repeat the wrongful action; or one may be merely embarrassed. The available alternatives are plentiful; and it is highly unlikely that the addition of any number of subclauses to the thought that is experienced with distress will succeed finally in ruling all of them out, so that only remorse is left; and this is to ignore the possibility of such perverse or inappropriate—though distressful—experiences as one might have of a given thought. So it seems that an emotion cannot be designated uniquely, even within a particular subclass of hedonic tone, by specifying the thought it involves, with whatever exactitude. Therefore it is necessary to turn our attention once more to the tone itself; for the only remaining strategy is to attempt a more exact characterization of *that*, if the emotion is at last to be picked out. But this presents us with a problem. For it is not possible to offer a more precise characterization of distress of a kind that will help us. Distress, like any other hedonic tone, may occur in varying degrees of intensity and for varying lengths of time; but to specify the values of these variables is not to designate remorse uniquely; for any distressful emotion can be more or less intense and more or less enduring. Yet specifications of this kind would appear to be the *only* additional specifications that we can offer of particular subclasses of hedonic tone—without, that is, by referring to the emotion which involves them ("remorseful distress," "joyous pleasure," "hubristic satisfaction" and so forth).

So it seems that remorse cannot be captured by the proposed model. Neither the thought nor the hedonic tone it involves can be specified sufficiently to designate it uniquely. Now by itself, again, this may mean no more than that remorse is an emotion which diverges to a certain degree from the model. But when we notice that the foregoing discussion might as easily have had any of the other distressful emotions for its subject, or have had some other subclass of hedonic tone for its purview, we must conclude that matters are more serious than this. For instead of functioning as a tiresome counterexample, the case of remorse in fact shows that *in general* hedonic tone is by itself too crude a notion adequately to supplement thought in a model of emotion; and we saw in the case of envy that not every emotion concept determines a hedonic tone. Therefore we should conclude that the place of hedonic tone in Budd's model of emotion has been exaggerated.[11] I suggest, then, that the following modification of his definition should be adopted: Emotions, which have specific experiential characters, are thoughts (often) expe-

---

11. A fact whose significance will become clear in Chapter 7.

rienced with certain forms of pleasure or pain, and (often) involving certain sensations or desires or behavioral dispositions. This is certainly less neat than Budd's formulation, but it is also more adequate. Had Budd been prepared to import into his model a disjunctive series of the kind that completes the revised version, envy would have posed him no problem, and remorse would have been specifiable by reference to the desires and behavioral dispositions it involves. Above all, the revised model avoids placing too heavy a burden on the notion of hedonic tone, which it is ill equipped to bear.

To conclude this section, then, let us again make use of Aristotle, this time in a manner suggested by Anthony Kenny.[12] When we experience emotion, we always experience emotion *about* something. This something is the object of our emotion. When I am afraid of your dog, or relieved by your failure, your dog and your failure are the *material objects* of my emotions. Any particular episode of emotion will take a material object; and as fear of your dog and fear of, say, botulism are apt to be dissimilar experiences, the character of each instance of emotion is logically dependent upon the nature of the material object taken. Fear of your dog and fear of botulism do, however, have this in common: in both cases the fear is a response to a perceived threat. "The threatening," then, is the *formal object* of fear, as "the welcome but not inevitable" is the formal object of relief. The formal object of an emotion gives the description which something must (be perceived to) satisfy if it is to be taken as the material object of an episode of that emotion. I cannot be relieved by what I perceive to be unwelcome or inevitable; nor can I fear what I perceive to be unthreatening. It will be seen from this that our discussion so far has dealt exclusively with formal matters; and, in particular, that the thoughts which, following Budd, have been construed as part of

12. Anthony Kenny, *Action, Emotion and Will* (London: Routledge and Kegan Paul, 1963), pp. 191–92.

each emotion have in fact had the formal objects of those emotions as their subjects. So, concerning remorse, the thought that one has acted wrongly gives "wrongful action by oneself" as the formal object of the emotion remorse. Now in particular episodes these thoughts of course concern the *material* object of emotion, so that the subject of the thought—for example, the thought of your failure—may give the material object of one particular episode of relief, that is, of relief at your failure. Therefore, to say that all emotions must involve a thought, and that all emotions must have an object, is to say the same thing; and in each case it is the *intentionality* of emotion that is underlined. So with our revised model of emotion in mind, and the distinction between formal and material objects established, we are now in a position to return to the matter left hanging at the end of Section II: what problems attend the various relations between music and the passions?

IV

We have seen that sensations would pose no problems (of the relevant kind); but I have shown that sensations are not passions, and I have suggested that none of the phenomena detailed in Sections I and II are sensations pure and simple. Therefore we must now consider the possibility that the passions discussed in those earlier sections are *emotions*. Let us begin with the passions of Section I. If *those* are emotions, we will be able at once to say where problems are apt to arise: wherever the material object of, or thought involved in, a putative episode of emotion is unclear; or wherever the material object, although identifiable, seems not to be able to satisfy the description it would have to satisfy in order to feature as the object of a putative episode of that particular emotion. What is at issue in the first case is whether the passion in question really is an emotion (for emotions have objects, involve thoughts); and in the second case, what description a certain kind of object—perhaps music, or musical performance—can satisfy.

It should be clear that most cognitive responses pose no problems in conforming to our model of emotion. For the objects of those emotions are the qualitative, quantitative and technical aspects of music, or of musical performance, and are thus identifiable in principle. Additionally, because those aspects are already picked out by description (as the beautiful, the long, the complex, etc.), they may appear as material objects of episodes of any emotion whose formal characterization is perceived to accommodate those descriptions. Thus, if I experience rapture at the beauty of a harmony, boredom at the length of a symphony, or disappointment at the complexity of a fugue, the objects of my emotions are the beauty of the harmony, the length of the symphony, and the complexity of the fugue; and I perceive these objects as falling under the descriptions "the wonderful," "the uninteresting" and "the unwelcome but not inevitable," respectively. Analogous remarks may be made of our cognitive responses to the handling, in composition or performance, of these various aspects. Problems occur only when the formal object of an emotion (e.g., of pity, "someone or something suffering") gives a description that a certain object cannot be thought to satisfy (e.g., the volume of a cadenza: for the volume of a cadenza cannot suffer). So some emotions cannot be experienced as cognitive responses to certain aspects of music; not can others as responses to the handling, in composition or performance, of those aspects: if I am neither the composer nor the performer, I cannot feel remorse for them, for instance. The prime philosophical problems that attend cognitive response, then, are these: how are the qualitative, quantitative and technical aspects of music to be determined; and which emotions can, in principle, be experienced in response to them. The first problem calls for extended theoretical treatment of quality in music, quantity in music and musical analysis, whereas the second calls for some detailed taxonomical work. For our present purposes, however, it is necessary to establish only that those cognitive responses to music which are properly construed as emotions are indeed emotions having certain aspects of music as their objects. And that, I believe, has been done.

Let us turn to sympathetic response—responses to the ex-press*ive* features of a musical work, where those features are not conceived as express*ing* anyone's passion. Sympathetic responses of a contrasting character to the expressive features oc-casioning them can be treated exactly like cognitive responses, so that they pose no problem in conforming to our model of emotion. Thus when I am perturbed by the depression or the high spirits of which a work, or its performance, is expressive, the depression or the high spirits are the objects of my emotion, and I conceive of those objects under the description "thought-provoking and mildly sinister" (one possible way of formulat-ing the formal object of perturbation). Likewise when I am perturbed by the manner in which these features are handled in composition or performance. The prime philosophical prob-lems that arise concern the capacity of music to be expressive of such states (i.e., what expressive features does music have, and *how* are they expressive?); and also some taxonomy. As before, I shall not be concerned with taxonomy. But of the first problem more will be said below, and indeed throughout.

We saw that sympathetic response can be *consonant,* as when we come to feel depressed at the depression of which Tchai-kovsky's Sixth Symphony is expressive. Now here it plainly need not be the case that the depression of which the music is expressive is the material object of *our* depression (as if we wished that the music were expressive of something else); we need not, in other words, think of the music's being expressive of that state as "something profoundly unpromising" (one pos-sible way of phrasing the formal object of depression). Rather, we may simply come to experience that state ourselves, as if by a kind of contagion. Nor is the material object of our depression whatever is the material object of the depression of which the music is expressive; for that depression is not conceived as a particular episode of (someone's) emotion. If this is the case then it would seem that such responses are not emotions; for emotions have objects, and if the object of our depression is neither the depression of which the music is expressive nor the object of *that* depression, then there would nevertheless appear to be nothing else that could count as its object: for there is nothing *in particular* that we need to conceive as profoundly unpromising in order thus to experience depression.

This last step is mildly controversial. There is some debate as to whether it makes sense to speak of passions which lack a clearly defined material object in the way that I have just suggested that depression might. However it is not as controversial as it once was. When the "cognitive" theory of emotion (a version of which is espoused here) was enjoying a renaissance in the 1960s and early 1970s, writers such as Anthony Kenny and J. R. S. Wilson seemed to be fairly adamant that passions without material objects were not to be countenanced; and certain philosophers seem still to agree.[13] But it was pointed out almost at once that this view was too dogmatic. In 1965 J. C. Gosling made a persuasive case for regarding particular instances of depression, and also of certain other passions, as genuinely objectless;[14] and he called such instances "moods" in order to distinguish them from emotions.[15] And it is Gosling's position that has become, if anything, the orthodoxy. Here, for instance, is Stephen Davies: "Kenny and Wilson treat responses lacking emotional-objects as rare and even aberrant. Whilst it can readily be conceded that, in the paradigm case, responses take emotional-objects, it may be that responses lacking

---

13. See Kenny, *Action, Emotion and Will;* J. R. S. Wilson, *Emotion and Object* (Cambridge: Cambridge University Press, 1972); and Peter Kivy in *Sound Sentiment* (Philadelphia: Temple University Press, 1989), p. 156—although Kivy seems to have modified his line since: see his "Auditor's Emotions: Contention, Concession and Compromise," *Journal of Aesthetics and Art Criticism* (1993): 1–12.

14. J. C. Gosling, "Emotion and Object," *Philosophical Review* (1965): 486–503.

15. A usage later favored by Mary Warnock and others—see her *Existentialism* (Oxford: Oxford University Press, 1970), p. 26.

emotional-objects are more common than they allow."[16] And in similar vein, but now relating the question specifically to the experience of music, here is Colin Radford: "My contention is that although the sadness of pure music can make us sad, i.e. we are saddened *by* it, we are not sad *about* the music or its sadness. . . . The music is the focus of our attention, its perceived sadness . . . makes us feel sad . . . , but we are not sad . . . about or for the music or its perceived emotional tone or property. . . . These feelings . . . lack objects, i.e. are not *about* anything."[17] I agree wholeheartedly with these writers; and I would urge anyone who is skeptical simply to reflect upon what it is like to get out of bed on the wrong side—to experience that feeling of free-floating depression and irritation. There is nothing *in particular* that one is depressed or irritated about—that is, there is nothing that appears to count as the material object of one's depression or irritation; and yet there is no question that one's state is real, and disagreeably real at that.

I shall call such states—states of passion that lack clearly defined material objects—*feelings* (a stipulative, technical definition). Feelings, then, are like emotions shorn of their cognitive aspect,[18] emotions that do not involve the thoughts about particular objects which make them episodes of this emotion rather than that. But what, in that case, distinguishes feelings from one another? What is the difference between a feeling of depression, for instance, and one of irritation? The answer is to be found in the idea of a *formal* object. If I get out of bed on the wrong side and experience feelings of depression, I regard

16. Stephen Davies, "The Rationality of Aesthetic Responses," *British Journal of Aesthetics* (1983): 46.

17. Colin Radford, "Muddy Waters," *Journal of Aesthetics and Art Criticism* (1991): 249–50; Radford has also argued this point in "Emotions and Music: A Reply to the Cognitivists," *Journal of Aesthetics and Art Criticism* (1989): 69–76.

18. Cf. Jerrold Levinson, who also recognizes the reality of such states: "Music and Negative Emotion," *Pacific Philosophical Quarterly* (1982): 327–46, reprinted in his collection *Music, Art, and Metaphysics* (Ithaca: Cornell University Press, 1990), pp. 306–35.

nothing in particular as fitting the description given by the formal object of the emotion depression; rather, I have a tendency to regard things in general as fitting that description. I regard more or less everything that I experience or think of as "profoundly unpromising." It is in this sense that such a feeling is "free-floating." Not being "about" anything in particular, it tends to light upon anything at all; and in this way it may be said to "color our world." A feeling, remarks Colin Radford, "does not have a particular object, target, or focus; it is quite general, global."[19] Indeed, there is some point to the thought that a feeling might best be treated as an all-encompassing kind of emotion, which simply takes "the world" or whatever is encountered in it as a globally material object; and this idea will be explored further in Chapter 7. But for the time being it is more important to underline the differences between emotions and feelings. Emotions take quite particular material objects, which are seen under the descriptions given by the relevant formal objects; feelings do not take particular material objects but instead consist in a tendency to regard things in general as fitting the descriptions given by the relevant formal objects. Thus if our depressed sympathetic response to the depression of which Tchaikovsky's Sixth Symphony is expressive is a feeling, then its lack of a material object is unproblematic. We need only, as a result of hearing the music, have a tendency to experience and respond to our world under a certain description, namely, the description given by the formal object of depression, the state of which we conceive the music to be expressive.

I shall assume, therefore, that sympathetic responses to music may be feelings, and I shall once again ignore questions of taxonomy, beyond noting that many emotions have co-nominal feelings: depression may be *either* an emotion *or* a feeling; so may sadness, cheerfulness, happiness, irritation and joy, among

19. Radford, "Muddy Waters," p. 250.

others. Not every emotion has a co-nominal feeling. And we will see later that this fact has implications for the range of passions of which music may be said to be expressive. But that is a matter to be dealt with in its proper place (which, again, is Chapter 7).

Empathetic and associative responses may now be treated quite quickly. The former, it will be remembered, are responses to what we take to be expressions of *someone's* passion. Contrasting empathetic responses therefore conform to our model of emotion exactly as cognitive and contrasting sympathetic responses did, the material objects taken by episodes of this kind of response being the person whose passion we take the music, or the performance of the music, to express. Consonant empathetic responses, on the other hand, may diverge from the pattern. For unlike consonant sympathetic responses, they may have objects and thus may not properly be classed as feelings. This is because if we *do* conceive the passion which the music expresses as *somebody's* passion, that passion, if it is an emotion, has an object: therefore, if we empathetically respond, and so come to feel *with* the person whose emotion is thought to be expressed, our response may have the same object as that person's emotion; and therefore, our empathetic response may itself be an emotion. Equally, of course, our response may be a feeling: for our responses need not take an object; we may not know what the emotion of the person to whom we respond has for object, and that person may be in some state, such as a state of feeling, which has no object. So consonant empathetic responses may be either emotions or feelings.

Associative responses may also be emotions or feelings— emotions, when whatever we associate the music with is the object of our response, or when the music is the object of our response in virtue of that association; and feelings, when reflection upon whatever we associate the music with leads us to experience our world under certain descriptions.

We have now seen that the passions to which music may

move us can be emotions, having many different kinds of material object, or perhaps feelings, which have none; and we should remember, as was noted at the end of Section I, that we may experience many of these responses at once, so that the emotions and feelings to which music may move us can be mixed and very complex. We have seen, too, that such problems as attend cognitive response are to be solved by the investigation of matters having no further direct bearing upon the passions; whereas other problems—those attending sympathetic and empathetic response—bear directly upon further matters of passion: that is, upon the expressive capacity of music, and its manner. It is to these latter that we must now briefly turn.

In Section II I remarked that just as sympathetic response depends upon the expressive capacity of music, so must empathetic response, for a musical work must first be heard as expressive before it can be heard as an expression. So expressiveness must in this sense be taken as basic. I also suggested in that section that expressiveness was related to passion in a "general sense," because no one's passion in particular was (necessarily) involved. Our subsequent discussion of emotion should now enable us to make a rather more detailed suggestion. For we have seen that every emotion (depression, perturbation, relief and so forth), as distinct from any episode of emotion (*this* depression, *this* perturbation), takes a formal object, by means of which the emotion-type may be identified without reference to any particular episode of it. The emotion-type can be picked out without being attributed to anyone. Emotions construed thus would appear to have just the generality we require. So the question is whether it makes any sense to speak of something being expressive of emotion thus construed (construed, in fact, as *feeling*). Consider the expressive face of someone whose genuine passions are not expressed therein—someone who, for instance, *practices* looking exultant, or looking terrified (let's call him Ralph). Now, on the one hand it is clear that no episodes of these emotions are going on and therefore that his expressive behavior expresses neither a passion of *his,* nor any passion having a material object. But, equally, it is clear that we can identify the *types* of passion of which his behavior is expressive. We might say Ralph's behavior was expressive of exultation, as at something fantastically welcome, or his behavior was expressive of terror, as at something tremendously threatening. In each case we make reference *only* to the formal object of the passion of which his behavior is expressive. In this sense, then, it is possible to speak of something's being expressive of an emotion-type, formally construed—which is to say that it is possible to speak of something's being expressive of a feeling.

Schopenhauer seems to have had something similar in mind for music when he said: "Music does not express this or that particular and definite pleasure, this or that affliction, pain, sorrow, horror, gaiety, merriment, or peace of mind, but joy, pain, sorrow, horror, gaiety, peace of mind *themselves,* to a certain extent in the abstract, their essential nature, without any accessories, and so also without the motives for them."[20] Should it turn out to be possible to speak of music being expressive in this formal sense, then it might also be possible to speak of music expressing passions that are someone's: for we have seen that expression depends upon expressiveness. And if both expressiveness and expression are possible, then the problems attending sympathetic and empathetic response will have been resolved. These are the matters that will occupy us, in large part, for the remainder of this book.

20. Arthur Schopenhauer, *The World as Will and Representation* (New York: Dover, 1969); 1:261.

CHAPTER TWO

Value and the Passions

He was there questioned as to whether he admitted that in
Christ there were two Natures after the Union, and that Christ
was consubstantial according to the flesh with us. After some
controversy he accepted the latter doctrine, but refused to
profess Christ's existence in two Natures. "Of two Natures—
but not *In* two Natures," he said.

Eutyches was therefore deposed and excommunicated.

—M. L. COZENS, *A Handbook of Heresies*

We have seen how diverse the relations between music and the
passions can be; and also that the passions can themselves be
diverse—sometimes emotions, sometimes feelings. But it is now
time to narrow the scope of our inquiry. If, when we listen to
music, our interest in the passions to which it is related is not
also and at the same time an interest in the music itself, then the
mere fact that the two are related in some way is of little
consequence to us. I suggested in the Introduction that an
inquiry such as this should contribute to a theory of musical
value, because its relation to passion is one of the things that we
value (some) music for. It follows from this that there should be
modes of relation between music and the passions which permit our valuation of passion to be tantamount to a certain form
of valuation of music. Otherwise the upshot of the inquiry will
be simply to produce a theory of *passionate* value. In Chapter 1
no attempt was made to discriminate between those relations
between music and passion that might feature in an account of
musical value and those that would not. This is the step that
must now be taken.

I

The attempt to come up with a description of the relation between music and passion so that an interest in the passion will be at the same time an interest in the music turns out to be a delicate one. Descriptions that fail in this are guilty of what Malcolm Budd has called "the heresy of the separable experience": the "separation of [the experience of] what gives music its value . . . from [the experience of] the music itself." In general, a heretical description "represents a musical work as being related in a certain way to an experience which can be fully characterized without reference to the nature of the work itself,"[1] so that insofar as this relation is concerned, the music functions simply as a means to an end, that end being an experience which is not ineliminably an experience of the music. No experience that can be fully characterized without reference to what occasions it is ineliminably an experience of that occasion; for exactly the same experience, identically characterized, can in principle be occasioned by something else. Therefore, if our experience of some given relation between music and passion is described such that the passion can be characterized (and valued) independently of the music to which it is related, it is in principle possible that there is something else (another piece of music, a drug, or whatever) that is related to that passion in the same way, and that is similarly efficient, or perhaps even more efficient, at providing access to it. The point here is not that music might in principle become dispensable and that this thought is unwelcome. For if a description of the relation between music and passion that has this consequence is a true description, then enthusiasm for that consequence is unnecessary. Rather, the point is that such a description could not be the *only* true one, for when we listen to some music the experience of (being put in mind of) certain passions is itself a

1. Malcolm Budd, *Music and the Emotions* (London: Routledge and Kegan Paul, 1985), p. 123.

mode of experiencing the music; so that there is just one experience to be described—an experience that cannot be described without reference to the music, because it is an experience *of* it. As Budd says: "When we are eager to listen to Elgar's *Violin Concerto* our reason is not that it happens to be the sole means for producing in us an experience which does not itself involve hearing the music: we value the experience of the music itself."[2]

Now, it should be clear from this that at least one of the relations between music and passion which we looked at in Chapter 1 cannot be used to underpin an account of passion in musical value. The passions that arise through *associative* response are fully characterizable without reference to the music that occasions them. Therefore, any account that seeks to explain the value of that music solely by reference to the value of the passions in associative response must necessarily be guilty of the heresy of the separable experience. We saw in Section I of the preceding chapter that an associative response is never grounded in any fact about the music itself, but rather is triggered by some contingent connection that the music has to persons or states of affairs, which persons or states of affairs are, when that response is an emotion, the *objects* of that response. Because the character of an episode of emotion—that is, of a certain experience—is determined by its object, and because the objects of associative response—for example, a past event, or a type of person—are describable independently of any music, it follows that the experience of an episode of such emotion is only eliminably an experience of any music. Therefore, whatever value attaches to that experience cannot be thought to attach to the music that is the occasion of it.

Certainly this consideration is sufficient to disqualify associative response as a source of musical value. But it shows also that any other mode of response whose object is characterizable

2. Ibid., p. 124.

without reference to the music occasioning it is inadmissible, and on identical grounds. Of the modes of response we have looked at, we can say this: cognitive responses, insofar as their objects are always aspects—whether qualitative, quantitative or technical—of the music itself, are admissable; although insofar as they are responses to aspects thought valuable on grounds other than the responses they give rise to—as, for example, the thrill at a complex rhythm may be a response to an aspect of the music, namely its rhythm, which would be valued whether or not the listener experiences a thrill, and perhaps would not be found thrilling were it not so valued—such responses may play only a secondary role of an account of passion in musical value. Contrasting sympathetic responses, because their objects are features—expressive features—of the music, must also be admissable in principle, although, again, their role may be secondary when what is responded to is valued on other grounds and would not have been the object of a given response were it not so valued. For example, the expressiveness of the brief *Adagio cantabile* in Beethoven's A-major Cello Sonata, Op. 69, while it would certainly not be so *relieving* were it not for the more rambunctious expressive character of the preceding two movements, would not be so *pleasing,* either, were that expressive contrast not valued in its own right. Thus, a particular contrasting sympathetic response—of relieved pleasure, say, at the expressiveness of Beethoven's *Adagio cantabile*—may be an experience of Beethoven's music that is valuable in its own right, and that also depends upon the value of Beethoven's music.

Consonant sympathetic responses, on the other hand, look a bit more tricky. For although in these responses we come to feel the passion of which a musical work is expressive, and therefore have an experience which depends upon the nature of that musical work, the work itself can nevertheless not be the *object* of our response if, as was suggested in Chapter 1, that response is a *feeling.* For feelings have no objects. The question, therefore, whether such an experience is a way of experiencing the *music* depends upon whether a feeling can be characterized without reference to what gives rise to it. If it can be so characterized, then consonant sympathetic response cannot by itself provide an account of passion in musical value. I shall address in detail the question whether this is so in Chapter 6. But let us note here that much rests upon the account we give of expressiveness; for the expressiveness of music is what gives rise to sympathetic response, and if the passions of which music is expressive are *merely* general ones (e.g., emotion-types, formally character-ized, as was suggested at the end of the preceding chapter), then consonant sympathetic responses are useless to us, for they depend upon musical features expressive of passions that are themselves fully characterizable without reference to the music expressive of them.

There would also seem to be problems with empathetic response—the kind of response upon which a good number of Romantic theories of expression-as-transmission depend. Tol-stoy held such a theory in the context of literature and paint-ing.[3] But for a specifically musical version, we do best to turn to Deryck Cooke.[4] Cooke presents the composer as having a cer-tain passionate experience that, by composing music expressive of the passion experienced, he transmits to the listener, so that the experience which the listener has as an empathetic response is (more or less) the same as the composer's original passion. There are difficulties with Cooke's proposed mechanism of transmission, however. He tries to compile a kind of dictionary of music's expressive vocabulary, in which thematic intervals and very short phrases are assigned allegedly invariant expres-sive functions (where expressiveness here is clearly a question of *conventional* expressiveness). A descending minor triad, for example, is held always to be expressive of "passive sorrow." But the necessary invariance simply doesn't exist—as the briefest

3. Leo Tolstoy *What Is Art?* (New York: Hesperides, 1962).
4. Deryck Cooke, *The Language of Music* (London: Faber, 1959).

reflection upon the opening of the *Appassionata*, or upon the huge numbers of other descending minor triads that have nothing at all to do with passive sorrow (or, for that matter, with one another), will show. One solution to this difficulty might be to select rather longer motifs and phrases as the units of expressive invariance, which—because they are likely to be encountered in fewer contexts—are less likely to find themselves buried instantly beneath an avalanche of counterexamples. Donald Ferguson has tried this tactic. He claims that "one motion-pattern retain[s], like a word-root affected by various prefixes and suffixes, a certain residual and apparently ineradicable value of suggestion";[5] and because his "motion-patterns" are sometimes several bars long, examples often bear him out. The scherzo theme of Schumann's Fourth Symphony, for instance, sounds all but a reworking in triple-time of the tune from the allegretto of Mozart's Piano Concerto K. 491. The themes certainly share something of the same, almost playful, expressive character, and the (significant) differences between the themes doubtless account for the comparatively carefree quality of the one, where the other is far more tense, and poised. But other examples are altogether less encouraging. The finale of Shostakovich's Fifteenth Symphony is studded with quotations from other people's works that—however expressive they may have been in their original places—are drained of all significance in this unattractive melange. Which strongly suggests that however stable the meanings of word-roots are between contexts, the expressive significances of musical phrases are less so. Ferguson's account, however, to which we shall return in Chapter 5, contains other, more valuable, suggestions and does not stand or fall with his lexical optimism. Cooke's, on the other hand, does; and *his* difficulties are exacerbated by his method. For he attempts to establish his expressive invariances inductively, by producing hundreds of supporting examples from the music of

5. Donald Ferguson, *Music as Metaphor* (Minneapolis: University of Minnesota Press, 1960), p. 106.

the last six centuries. But as Michael Tanner has pointed out, "Unless one were able to tell in a single case that a minor ninth had diabolic connotations, the multiplication of cases would have no confirmatory force; and if one can tell in a single instance that that property does inhere in a minor ninth, further examples are redundant."[6]

Yet even if neither of these difficulties was decisive, the transmission theory would still be unacceptable in anything like this form. For it construes music as a means to an end—as a means for transmitting to the listener a passion that the composer experiences quite independently of the music he then composes to be expressive of it; which indicates that other means might in principle serve as adequately; which suggests that neither composer nor listener has an experience that is ineliminably an experience of the music.[7] So transmission theories such as Cooke's are guilty of the heresy of the separable experience.

But transmission theories (thus construed) do not exhaust the possibilities inherent in empathetic response, as I will try to show in Chapter 8. Part of the reason for this is that they depend in the first place upon sympathetic response: for it is unclear that the experience of the listener need be related in any way (by the listener) to the experience allegedly undergone by the composer (even if it is granted that it is the composer's experience that the music transmits). The listener need not in principle come to conceive the music as an expression, only as expressive. But a stronger appeal to empathetic response is still problematic. For when these responses are emotions their objects are either the person whose passions the music is taken to be expressive of, or the objects of *that* person's passions. In neither case is the object of response the music; and nor, as yet, is there any reason to suppose that a description of either of these responses will involve ineliminable reference to the music occa-

---

6. Michael Tanner, "Understanding Music," *Proceedings of the Aristotelian Society* (Supplementary vol., 1985): 224.
7. As Budd also points out in *Music and the Emotions*, p. 123.

sioning them. So for the time being we shall put empathetic response aside. We can note again, however, that much depends upon the account that we give of expressiveness; for expression depends on expressiveness, and if our empathetic responses to expression depend upon musical features expressive of passions fully characterizable without reference to the music expressive of them, then such responses are inadmissable. This is one of the reasons why we must now begin to devote ourselves to questions surrounding musical expressiveness; and we will start by asking how the experience of such expressiveness might be characterized in a nonheretical way.

II

The considerations offered in the previous section suggest that descriptions guilty of the heresy of the separable experience multiply inappropriately the experiences that listening to music comprises. The mode of attention involved in such listening is incorrectly described so that more than one *act* of attention is essential, and thus so that the experience of the passions to which the music is related is separated from the experience of the music itself. One way around this difficulty might be to suppose that a successful, nonheretical account is to be founded upon a strong commitment to the unity of those objects of attention which heretical accounts, in their multiplication of attentive *acts,* tend to render disparate—to suppose, in other words, that the separable experience is to be avoided by recourse to the indivisibility of the object of experience, so that a right apprehension of the object will *entail* an appropriate experience of it.

The unity of musical aspects (here, in particular, the expressive and nonexpressive aspects) has always exerted a strong attraction over those engaged in theorizing about music. For some, indeed, the attraction has been so strong that the successful unification of such aspects in a musical work confers upon that work a moral significance. Hindemith, for example, asserts that "a tremendous effort is necessary in order to work towards it [unity]; not merely a technical effort, but a moral effort, too— the effort to subject all considerations of technique, style and purpose to this one ideal, [in which everything] . . . is in congruence with the . . . vision." Those who have not the "moral energy" to maintain the "Augustinian attitude," who "consider a search for beautiful details justifiable," are akin to the philatelist, "who with all his efforts succeeds merely in getting together a collection, never in creating an organism."[8] The Augustinian composer will therefore no more be impressed by the listener who admires his collection at the expense of the organism he has created than he will praise the composer of beautiful details. The Augustinian stricture of course applies more firmly to composers than it does to listeners. It requires, for example, that the composer never sacrifice the longer view of his work to the shorter. But equally, insofar as the composer has been successful in this, there is made available to and perhaps even imposed upon the listener an attitude that is the counterpart of the composer's—an attitude that takes and comprehends the musical work as a unity. In a similar way, a piece of advice from Copland to "young composers" can be interpreted from the listener's point of view. He recommends "a full and equal appraisal of every smallest contributing factor, with an understanding of the controlling and most essential elements in the piece, without allowing this to cramp one's freedom of creative inventiveness—being, as it were, inside and outside the work at the same time." Copland includes among his contributing factors "psychological and emotional connotations."[9]

Copland does not offer any further explication of the unity of "emotional connotations" with other "contributing factors"; and Hindemith, as we shall see in Chapter 6, has a rather

8. Paul Hindemith, *A Composer's World* (Cambridge: Harvard University Press, 1952), pp. 62–64.

9. Aaron Copland, *Music and Imagination* (Cambridge: Harvard University Press, 1952), p. 45.

peculiar, and not strikingly Augustinian, view about the relation between music and passion—one, indeed, that requires very tactful exposition if it is not to run afoul at once of the heresy of the separable experience. The most resourceful and Augustinian attempt to describe the unification of those musical aspects with which we are concerned is to be found in Busoni's *Sketch of a New Aesthetic of Music*. Busoni tries to give an account of style in terms of feeling (style being another of the considerations that the Augustinian composer subjects ruthlessly to the ideal of "congruence with the vision"), so that musical expressiveness becomes *identified* with style. He says that "style forms itself out of feeling when led by taste," so that music "repeats the feelings of life."[10] A sincere taste, he thinks, for these feelings (or for a set of them) is a precondition of a genuine style, and it is style which is the distinctive feature of art.

Busoni's formulation seems very flexible. It allows him to account for differences between the styles of individuals, between national styles, and between styles characteristic of particular periods. His formulation is also quite clearly influenced by an Augustinian predilection for unity. Because for him part of the business of music is the repetition of the "feelings of life," those feelings constitute at least part of the content, or constitute one aspect, of the music. And because it is from tastes for a certain kind of feeling that a style is formed, that content is ineliminably part of what a given style is, and the style cannot be accounted for or understood without reference to it. For any true feeling for which the composer has a sincere taste there is an answering style. That style is not merely suitable, as if some other might in principle have served as well; it is a *function* of the favored feeling. Therefore, an interest in the feelings "repeated" by a particular musical work is ineliminably an interest in the style characteristic of it; and thus, because the style of a

10. Ferruccio Busoni, *Sketch of a New Aesthetic of Music* (New York: Dover, 1962), p. 98.

work cannot be thought of without reference to that work, an interest in those feelings must ineliminably be an interest in the nature of the music itself. The heresy of the separable experience would seem to have been avoided.

It would also appear to be a strength of Busoni's formulation that it is symmetrical. For not only is it the case that style follows feeling; it must also be true that a composer who has established for himself a style from which he does not incline, or is not able, to deviate has at the same time determined which feelings his music will be able to "repeat." Feeling follows style, then, as well. When Chopin composed the third movement of his Piano Sonata in B minor, his style was not even potentially capable of the feeling that informs the *Marcia funebre* of the *Eroica*. On the one hand we have a kind of self-communing misery, and on the other the most solemn grief. It is inconceivable that Chopin's manner could have accommodated Beethoven's passion (or, more strictly, the passion of which Beethoven's music is expressive). Busoni's thoughts on style appear to offer some explanation for this and, similarly, for the corresponding fact that the listener who wishes to grasp the passions of which a piece of music is expressive must also grasp the style in which it is composed. Any useful account of style must have something to say about these matters. Further, Busoni has no problem in accounting for changes in the style of a given composer: he need merely say that at some point the composer conceived a sincere taste for a true feeling that had previously not appealed to him, after an earlier period of having had a real taste for some other feeling that then ceased to appeal to him. Style is a function of the favored feeling, and alters as the favors are redistributed.

But for all these apparent advantages, Busoni's account is nonetheless quite unsustainable. It seems to set up an uncontrollable dialectic, in which either style or feeling becomes lost, depending upon which of these two aspects is particularly emphasized. If feeling is particularly emphasized then the concept of style is deprived of all content. We might regard expressive *variety*, for example, as a feature of a composer's style; and it may often be the contrast of expressive ends *within* a piece that is the focus of the listener's interest (as in Beethoven's Ninth Symphony, for instance, or in almost any truly *dramatic* opera). But on Busoni's account such variety and contrast would necessarily entail stylistic heterogeneity; for each different feeling of which a work was expressive would "form" its own specific style. And similarly, if style really *were* formed out of feeling, we would expect that the style of Beethoven in pastoral mood would strongly resemble that of, say, Delius in a similar frame of mind. But a moment's reflection upon the respective manners of the Sixth Symphony and *On Hearing the First Cuckoo in Spring* shows how implausible such a claim would be; for nonpastoral Beethoven is infinitely more of a style with pastoral Beethoven than is Delius in any mood whatever. To emphasize feeling in this way is to render style so tyrannized that it loses its meaning entirely; and since it was because an interest in a work's style was ineliminably an interest in the work itself that the heresy of the separable experience was to be avoided, an *empty* conception of style will go no way toward the sought-after unification of music's expressive aspects with its nonexpressive aspects. This emphasis is therefore fatal to Busoni's account.

But a contrasting emphasis on style will not improve matters—though Busoni himself seems sometimes to favor such an emphasis: there may be an "attempt to express . . . feeling in little, in detail, for a short stretch"; but, fearing no doubt that the philatelist looms large in this, he will have nothing of it. He dismisses such attempts as the province of the amateur or mediocre artist and contrasts with this style his own: "Feeling on the grand scale," he says, "is mistaken . . . for want of emotion, because . . . [people] are all unable to hear the longer reaches as parts of a yet more extended whole."[11] (This is

11. Ibid.

interestingly similar to something Schoenberg once said: "I myself consider the totality of a piece as the *idea*"—where by "idea" he means, among other things, *expressive* idea; the composer "will never start from a preconceived image of a style; he will be ceaselessly occupied with doing justice to the idea. He is sure that, everything done which the idea demands, the external appearance of it"—that is, the style—"will be adequate."[12]) So Busoni's style is formed out of a feeling that reveals itself only in the whole work (for even very long reaches are still only parts of the whole). But it must therefore be the case that every work has its own feelings *and* its own style, which is to say nothing about either. For on this construction, to say that Busoni's Piano Concerto is expressive of a feeling or is in a style is just to say that it is the work that it is; and to say that another work is in the *same* style or is expressive of the *same* feeling is just to say that there exists another(?) work that is identical to Busoni's Piano Concerto in every respect. And this is certainly not to provide such an account of the relation between music's expressive and nonexpressive aspects as will ground a nonheretical description of the former; for *no* description, heretical or otherwise, of the "feeling" of which a work is expressive is now available.

It seems, then, that a successful and nonheretical account of the relation between music and passion ought not to be founded upon this kind of commitment to the indivisibility of the object of experience. For either the association is eliminated (when *feeling* is emphasized) and heresy made unavoidable; or the passions are eliminated (when style, or the "yet more extended whole," is emphasized) and the problem simply wished away. So although Busoni was surely right to argue that music's expressive and nonexpressive aspects must be intimately related, he was wrong to attempt to define those aspects in terms of one another. Or, to put the matter in terms of *performance* (the context, after all, in which the listener has the experience

12. Arnold Schoenberg, *Style and Idea* (London: Faber, 1975), pp. 121–23.

nonheretically to be described): although it must surely be true that the specific expressive character of a performance of a musical work will (and indeed must) contribute to and depend upon the nature of that performance as a whole—and although it must surely be the case that, because the nature of a performance of a work depends upon and is constrained by the nature of the work itself, the expressive character of a particular work must contribute to and depend upon the nature of that work— it is nonetheless not useful to attempt to *identify* its expressive character with other aspects of the work (or performance), or with that work (or performance) as a whole. Busoni's theory constitutes, and illustrates the shortcomings of, one such attempt. In trying to produce a nonheretical account of the relation between music and the passions, we must develop some rather different tactics; and to that I shall devote the next chapter.

CHAPTER THREE

Understanding Music

And he hearkened diligently with much heed.

—Isaiah 21.7

In the preceding chapter we saw how one attempt to avoid the heresy of the separable experience came to grief. What we need is some way of characterizing the experience of listening to music so that the expressive and the nonexpressive aspects of it are the objects of some *single* act of attention. If we get this right, then the motive for attempting too tightly to yoke those aspects together, as Busoni tried to do, will have been removed; and we shall have taken a significant step toward the conclusion that at least some music is valuable *in virtue of* the expressive aspects it contains. Now the experience of listening to music so that both expressive and nonexpressive aspects are taken account of is an experience of *understanding* music in a certain way, and it will be within the range of the possible objects of *that* experience that those modes of relation between music and the passions most germane to a theory of musical value will be found. So what is it to listen to music with understanding?

I

One can say straight away that in order to hear music with understanding it is essential to understand that what one is hearing is music—to hear what one hears, in other words, *as*

music, and not merely as an auditory stimulus of some unspecified kind, or as noise. But it is not immediately obvious what
this (rather rudimentary) form of understanding might involve.
In a recent article, Kingsley Price assumes that what is understood when music is understood as music must be a *meaning* of
some kind; and for the variety of meaning that he has in mind
Price makes the following surprising claim: "Its objectivity and
determinateness make the immanent meaning of music a better
paradigm for those who would discover the nature of meaning
in general than does the meaning found in language."[1]

The kind of meaning that he thinks music has it has in virtue
of its "phenomenological intelligibility"—that property which
the sentence " 'Twas brillig and the slithy tove did gyre and
gimble in the wabe" has, and which the sentence " 'Twas did
gyre, the and gimble slithy tove in and wabe brillig the" lacks. Of
the words in Carroll's original line, we are "conscious of their
intelligible shapes as including the intelligible shapes of such
other words as they fit or refuse to fit with. . . . Their intelligible shapes contain, as well, a demand that words with the
shapes included should occur elsewhere in the sentence"[2]—
which means, I think, that Carroll's original sentence is syntac-
tically well formed and is felt to be so; and the question of
meaning arises because wherever we detect syntax we expect
also to find semantics. Music exhibits "phenomenological intelligibility," claims Price, because "one tone demands another":
the seventh degree of the scale demands the tonic just above it;
the subdominant demands the mediant. Mere pitched sound
makes no such demands, he thinks; it exhibits no "phenomenological intelligibility." "Phenomenological intelligibility" is thus
distinctive of music and allows it to be separated off from the
other possible objects of auditory experience. Tonality is the
condition of the "demanding" characteristic of music, so that

1. Kingsley Price, "Does Music Have Meaning?" *British Journal of Aesthetics*
(1988): 214.
2. Ibid., p. 205.

within tonal music the satisfaction or frustration of such demands (of tones for each other) is what makes a melody coherent or incoherent. To hear a pitch as the seventh in the scale
is to hear a tone which demands that the tonic should follow
soon, a demand which does not lapse when the tonic fails so to
follow, but rather persists, spanning whatever tones succeed the
seventh to yield an entire succession that without the tonic is
incoherent, and that with the tonic *is* coherent. Where there is
such a melody, a coherent tonal melody, there is, says Price,
"phenomenological intelligibility." And the species of meaning
grasped by the listener to whom the phenomenon is intelligible
is "immanent" meaning:

> We may distinguish two factors in the demand one tone makes
> for another—what is demanded (the other tone) and the de-
> manding of it. The second is a reference. The demanding of
> something must refer to what is demanded. Now the tone
> demanded is present in the demanding tone even though it has
> not yet occurred, or, as in incoherent melodies, may not occur at
> all; and since, in the most general sense of "meaning," one thing
> means another provided that the other is present in the one
> though absent from it, any tone means those tones which it
> includes and demands. Since this meaning is the meaning of
> tones, it does not transcend music, but is immanent in it. . . .
> [This meaning is objective, since] it is the tone that means, not
> the person who hears the tone . . . ; [and it is determinate,
> because] the tones demanded admit of no variation in pitch.[3]

Now there is a great deal in this passage with which one
might take issue. It is far from clear, for instance, whether
meaning is a term properly to be invoked in contexts of this
kind.[4] But even if meaning *were* the apposite term, there would
remain other, much more serious, objections. For Price a mel-

3. Ibid., p. 214.
4. R. A. Sharpe argues that it is not: see "Music: The Information-Theoretic
Approach," *British Journal of Aesthetics* (1971): 385–401.

ody is coherent insofar as the demands of its tones for other tones to follow is satisfied. So to hear a tone as demanding another tone is a way of hearing that tone with understanding as part of a piece of putatively coherent music. A tone *not* so heard cannot be grasped by the listener in the same way (it is heard merely as a pitch, perhaps). Therefore any coherent melody in which the demand of one tone for another is not immediately satisfied must contain sequences whose members are not heard by the understanding listener as part of that coherent melody—those sequences that come between the demanding tone (e.g., a seventh) and the tone demanded (e.g., the tonic). At best, such sequences will be grasped by the listener as part of *another* putatively coherent melody. Thus, in the melody of "Somewhere over the Rainbow," the tones (pitches?) on which the syllables -*ver the rain*- occur either are superfluous or else constitute another (incoherent) melody. Additionally, since the tonic makes no demands at all, being the rest tone onto which other tones resolve, the appearance of the tonic within a tune means that the tune is instantly coherent if there has been a seventh before the tonic, and also that the tonic makes no contribution to the coherence of any part of the tune that succeeds it; indeed, the parts that follow it are parts of a *new* melody from the point of view of coherence. So the melody of "Somewhere over the Rainbow" begins to count only when it gets off the tonic—that is, on the syllable *o*- of *over*. It follows from this that one hears with understanding the first line of the melody when one hears every note but the third and seventh notes—the *o*- of *over*, and the -*bow* of *rainbow*—as beside the point. Or, more generally, that to hear tonal music with understanding is to ignore the overwhelming majority of it.

In having this absurd conclusion forced upon him, Price has failed to see that we hear certain tones as "demanding" one another only *because* we hear them as part of a tonal melody. For although it is true in a weak sense that a seventh, for example, demands that the tonic follow soon, it is strings of tones—melodic segments—that make the strongest demands about what should follow, and the demands get stronger the longer the segments are. If a melody is broken off after its second note—even when that note is a seventh—the demands are weaker than if the melody is broken off after, say, its fourteenth note, whatever its fourteenth note is. By setting up his notion of "phenomenological intelligibility" in terms of linguistic syntax, in which small units (i.e., words), on his account, demand what kind of words should follow them (e.g., adjectives, nouns), and then by transferring this notion directly onto music, Price has given the smallest units of music (i.e., tones) quite the wrong significance, and has badly misconstrued the experience of listening to music with understanding as a result. He has in fact given an incorrect description of what it would be for language to aspire to the condition of music—although not a description that Pater or the Symbolists would have had a lot of time for, because the only difference between this kind of language and the ordinary sort is the absence of transcendental reference; and the perfect example of that already exists: " 'Twas brillig and the slithy tove . . ." What Pater and the Symbolists meant was, to be sure, language with significant immanent meaning; but also language that coheres in the way that music does, and not in the way that Price says language does.

But if Price is wrong to make the fundamental object of musical experience the single tone, he is surely right to want to distinguish the sounds that we hear when we hear them as part of a piece of music from those we hear when we hear them as *mere* pitched sound. For the experience of hearing music is not the same as that of hearing sounds. A melody is not *merely* a series of pitched sounds, nor is a rhythm a mere succession of louder and quieter sounds. Rather, in each case, listeners who understands what they're hearing hear the sounds *as* a melody, or *as* a rhythm, so that their understanding is a *way* of hearing certain successions and clusters of pitched and unpitched sounds as tones, rhythms, melodies, harmonies and so forth.

Roger Scruton has brought out this distinction with the help of a dove. Doves aren't deaf; they are presumably able to perceive the sounds of which their distinctive "cooing" noises consist— and yet there is no reason to think that they can hear in these sounds the 5/8 rhythm so striking to us: "If [a dove] heard that rhythm, would he not be persuaded of the merits of another? What is there in his behaviour which requires explanation in such terms? . . . It seems impossible to envisage what a dove's behaviour would have to be like for us to attribute to him . . . the perception of rhythm."[5] We ourselves, by contrast, are capable of hearing in a single aural stimulus—the sound of a train on its track, for instance—either a clattering racket or a rhythmic series of beats. The only change is in the *way* we hear what we hear, so that when we come to hear in a succession of sounds a rhythm rather than a racket we come to understand those sounds *as* a rhythm, whereas before we had understood them as a racket or perhaps not understood them at all. Scruton calls the sounds themselves the *material* objects of our musical experience, and the rhythm or the racket that we hear them *as,* the *intentional* objects of our musical experience. But we may prefer to capture the distinction without recourse to the language of intentional objects and say instead something like this: the experience of mere sound is an experience having *sensory* properties only; whereas the experience of sound as a rhythm or racket is an experience having *perceptual* properties also (where a perceptual property is a sensory property interpreted under some description—e.g., as music, as rhythm, as melody).[6] Thus, to hear music *as* music is to have an experience of a certain

5. Roger Scruton, *The Aesthetic Understanding* (London: Methuen, 1983), p. 90.

6. This distinction is similar (I think) to Christopher Peacocke's distinction between representational properties and sensational properties—see *Sense and Content* (Oxford University Press, 1983), chapter 1. See also Malcolm Budd, "Understanding Music," in *Proceedings of the Aristotelian Society* (Supplementary vol., 1985): 244.

kind—an experience of an intentional object of a particular sort (e.g., an object having melody, harmony, rhythm) or an experience possessing particular perceptual properties (e.g., melody, harmony, rhythm); and to understand music (in this rudimentary sense) is to be able to have experiences of this kind—is, in other words, to be able to hear the music in a certain *way*.

II

Now clearly this is only a rudimentary form of understanding; but its potential for sophistication and complexity is considerable. In particular, it should be noted that the various different kinds of perceptual property (melody, harmony etc.) may combine in an experience of a musical work so that some or all those properties are modified by their interrelations with the others. Thus, differing timbres may affect the degree of harmonic consonance or dissonance which identical sets of simultaneously sounded pitches are experienced as having. And these combinatory effects can be striking. The melodic interval at the final cadence of Sibelius's Seventh Symphony is a simple rising minor second, the smallest interval for which the traditional scale allows; and yet here, owing to the timbre, tempo and harmony of the passage (and perhaps also to other factors), the interval seems far greater. This is not to say that the interval might be *mistaken* for a greater interval (e.g., a third or a fifth), only that it is experienced as comprising a greater pitch difference than a minor second is usually experienced as comprising. Sibelius's cadence makes the adjacent semitone seem a very long way off indeed: for the perceptual property of melody is altered by the other perceptual properties that an experience of this music has.

It should be noted in addition that the perceptual properties the experience of a musical work may have are shaped and constrained not only by the nature of the object of the experience (e.g., which sounds it contains) but also by the condition of the listener whose experience it is. Thus, two listeners who hear a musical work *as* music—and whose experiences therefore share a certain minimum set of perceptual properties—may nevertheless differ in what further perceptual properties their experiences have, according to their differing capacities and dispositions, and to the varying degrees in which their previous experiences are related to the object of their current experience. A tired or inattentive listener, or a listener whose rhythmic sense is relatively poor, may hear two passages as having the same rhythm, whereas a more alert or gifted listener hears a rhythmic difference. So one *kind* of perceptual property (e.g., rhythm) may be possessed by an experience to varying degrees. But in addition, it may be that one listener's experience altogether lacks a perceptual property that is possessed by a second listener's. Sometimes this is a drawback: if the first listener fails to hear in Sibelius's cadence an unusually large distance between pitches a minor second apart, then something important in the music has been missed. But it need not always be the case that the experience of the first listener is an inadequate experience of the music, or even that that experience is the less desirable. Mozart's Fortieth Symphony, for instance, exists in two very slightly different versions. The earlier version is scored for an orchestra without clarinets, whereas the second version, re-scored by Mozart for a different occasion, has clarinets added in. Now, the experience of someone listening to the earlier version, if that is the only version known to that person, differs from that of a listener also familiar with the later version, in that the first listener's experience does not have clarinetlessness of timbre as a perceptual property. The listener does not *expect* clarinets (many symphonies of the period were scored without them), and thus does not hear their absence as a distinct quality of timbre. For such a listener, the clarinetlessness of the sound (like, for example, its saxophonelessness) is merely a sensory property of the experience of it. The listener familiar with both versions of the symphony, by contrast, will hear the clarinetlessness of the earlier version differently: its clarinetlessness will feature in a way that its saxophonelessness does not—as a perceptual and not merely a sensory property of the experience. This listener will hear clarinetlessness as a distinct quality of timbre.

III

From a very rudimentary form of understanding we have arrived, then, at something a little more elaborate. We have seen, for instance, that some perceptual properties may be rather subtle (as when the *absence* of an instrument is heard as a distinct quality of timbre); and we have seen that perceptual properties may modify one another. But it should be noted that the properties which an experience *must* have if it is to count (minimally) as an experience of music have been left vague, or merely gestured at (melody, rhythm, harmony etc.). And this is because music is of many different kinds. To hear a drum solo as rhythmic is doubtless to have an experience with at least one appropriate perceptual property. But to hear it as melodic also is (usually) to misunderstand it—that is, to have an experience with at least one inappropriate perceptual property. And in a similar way medieval monody is not normally understood if heard harmonically, nor a bagpipe's drone if heard as a rhythm. We cannot, I think, give any single necessary condition for hearing music as music. But in each of these cases we can at least see which properties are essential to a minimally musical experience of the sounds: if the sounds comprise an unpitched series, then we will be interested in rhythm; if pitches sounded together, then in harmony—and so forth. For the overwhelming majority of the music that most of us listen to, melody, rhythm and harmony each play some part in a minimally musical experience.

The question now arises: what *else* must figure if an experience is to be more than minimally musical? What is the deficiency in the experience of someone who can distinguish Mozart from roadworks, but not from Mahler? This person understands music in the rudimentary sense; but we should deny that the listener understood the music of Mozart. It would seem that the perceptual properties of such an experience are in some sense inadequate; they do not, in other words, comprise *all* the properties necessary for an understanding of Mozart's music. I suggest, therefore, that truly understanding listeners are listeners with the capacity and disposition to adjust the *way* they hear to what they hear, where such adjustment is not, or is not simply, a matter of the accumulation or intensification of perceptual properties (in simple music, after all, such accumulation or intensification may lead only to a pretentious understanding). The perceptual properties need to be the right properties, and their intensities must be apt. But to say which ones and how intense in any particular case is very difficult indeed. Certainly we cannot settle the matter merely by appealing to the *kinds* of sounds that a work involves, for such appeal will tell us no more than which properties are essential to a minimal experience: from the fact that medieval monody comprises only a series of nonsimultaneously sounded pitches we can infer that a melodic sense is necessary for (at least) a minimal experience of medieval monody. But we cannot infer (what is also true) that a harmonic sense is superfluous or distracting in such music, for when we listen to a Bach cello suite—which also comprises only a series of nonsimultaneously sounded pitches—we find that we cannot grasp it properly *without* a harmonic sense. So the fact that such a sense is not necessary for listening to medieval monody cannot be due simply to the sounds of which it consists (indeed, there's nothing to *stop* one from listening to it harmonically) but must be due, rather, to something in the listener's attitude which makes desirable the suspension of such a sense.

This something, surely, is a preference for satisfying or coherent experience. That we do have such preferences I take to be uncontroversial. Anyone who has ever looked at an unjoined-up join-the-dots picture or at one of M. C. Escher's visual paradoxes knows how keen we are to impose a coherent order on what we perceive, and how disconcerted we are when we find that we cannot. But by what means, or by reference to what, we realize a desire for a coherent experience of a complex auditory artifact like a Bach cello suite may be less clear. The first thing to say, probably, is that two people who both have a coherent experience of the same object may not experience that object in the same way. The object may be ambiguous. Also, certain people may simply have quirky or eccentric ways of imposing a coherent order on what they perceive. I don't think we can rule out cases of this kind; and consequently I don't think we can give any monolithic account of what it is for a musical experience to be coherent. But the possibility of quirky or eccentric ways of imposing order on an experience does at least suggest that there must also be a typical or nondeviant way of doing so. How might we try to capture that? Plainly we cannot simply define a typically coherent experience as one that is more than minimally musical—or not if we want to retain for the account anything recognizable as content. What we need is a relatively independent standard against which the coherence of a musical experience can typically be gauged. This, I think, we must get by appealing to historical and cultural convention. A typically coherent experience of a piece of music is, on this account, one that is in accord with whatever are the historically and culturally appropriate conventions for listening to music of the relevant kind. Thus such an experience includes an awareness of the music as having been produced in a particular music-historical context, to which certain habits of listening may be more or less appropriate. When these habits are appropriate, the experience they yield, other things being equal, is a coherent one. Now of course there is a faint whiff of circularity about this. But no one should find that surprising or alarming, much less vicious. For an element of circularity is just what one would expect when analyzing the reciprocal relations between the experience and the creation of the objects definitive of any relatively autonomous institution or tradition.[7] I suggest, then, that the standard against which the coherence of a musical experience should typically be gauged is to be found in those conventions which were historically relevant to the creation of the particular music experienced—which of course implies, not at all counterintuitively, that the more historically informed one's listening is, the more apt one is to experience coherently what one hears.

The reason then, why you typically don't want a harmonic sense engaged when you listen to medieval monody is that such a sense is historically and culturally inappropriate for listening to music of that kind, which in practice means there's nothing much there for the harmonic sense to get hold of and that what there is is unlikely to make your experience more intelligible. So on the one hand you'll find the music boring, because what you're looking for is largely absent; and on the other you'll find it confusing, because the little you do manage to find turns out not to have the implications you expect (or indeed any implications at all). So for the experience of medieval monody an active harmonic sense is a liability. If listeners find it undesirable or impossible to suspend that sense in their musical experience, then such music will be frustrating and tedious for them, and it will have been made so by their anachronistic listening habits. In listening to a Bach cello suite, by contrast, the harmonic sense is rewarded—the habit of listening harmonically is historically warranted. The monophonic lines *imply* harmonic progression, so that the experience of the listener who hears them harmonically has a dimension of coherence that a nonharmonic experience of those lines would lack. Thus, it is the preference for a certain kind of experience—a coherent and, typically, music-historically appropriate experience—that determines which perceptual properties must figure if an experi-

7. Compare, for instance, the similarly harmless whiff of circularity emanating from Jerrold Levinson's definition of art: "Defining Art Historically," *British Journal of Aesthetics* (1979): 232–50, reprinted in Levinson's *Music, Art, and Metaphysics* (Ithaca: Cornell University Press, 1990).

ence is to be more than minimally musical; and it is to the extent that listeners are capable of realizing this preference (even if they do so by quirky or nonstandard means) that they understand the music they listen to. Therefore the person who cannot distinguish Mozart from Mahler is, in a straightforward sense, incompetent—either to realize such a preference or maybe even (if *utterly* uninterested in music) to conceive it.

On this construction of musical understanding, then, understanding listeners get the perceptual properties of their experience right, standardly through the adoption of certain historically appropriate listening habits (which they may acquire by practice, by trial and error, by induction or whatever). And when they attempt to indicate what those properties are, they are engaging in music criticism.[8] For some music, doubtless, *no* set of properties answers fully—in which case the music is relatively incoherent. But in addition, some *performances* of otherwise coherent music may be impossible to experience with the appropriate perceptual properties—in which case the performances *make* the music incoherent. So to understand a (performance of a) piece of music is to be able to hear it in a certain way, is to be able to have an experience of it that has certain appropriate perceptual properties. I suggested at the beginning of this chapter that if the experience of listening to a musical work with understanding could be characterized so that the heresy of the separable experience was avoided, the motive for trying to homogenize the *objects* of that experience, as Busoni tried to do, would have been removed. We are now very nearly in a position to make this claim good. For the characterization just offered, because it concentrates upon the properties of a *single* (complex) experience—the experience of listening to music—does not multiply that experience or make its elements heretically separable. (It is for this reason that I have adopted the sensory-perceptual terminology. Scruton's

8. As Budd also remarks—see "Understanding Music," p. 245.

talk of intentional objects could have been made to serve, no doubt; yet it seems more economical to speak of an experience than of an intentional object that a material object is experienced as being, especially because it would then have to be shown that an intentional object is unitary. Speaking instead of the various aspects of the experience of an object quite properly leaves open what relations obtain between the various parts of the object itself.) But I have said nothing so far about expressiveness. My suggestion, of course, is that expressiveness can be construed as another of the kinds of perceptual property which an experience of music may have and which may therefore be included in the unobjectionable characterization of that experience given above. I shall now attempt to substantiate this suggestion; and, in doing so, to say a little more about the nature of musical understanding.

IV

It is clearly in the *unfolding* and the *progression* of a musical experience that most of its perceptual properties arise—both the basic ones (such as melody or rhythm) and the more subtle ones (such as at the final cadence of Sibelius's Seventh Symphony, or harmonic implication in a Bach cello suite). Listeners are thus engaged throughout in trying to make sense of, to understand, the unfolding and progression of their musical experience. They are likely to be successful in this attempt to the extent that the kind of music they listen to is familiar to them; for if it is very familiar then they are likely to have gained a grasp of whatever listening habits are historically appropriate; if it is very unfamiliar, by contrast, then the relevant habits are unlikely to have been acquired, and the progression of the experience will probably baffle. The listener who *can* make sense of the progression of an experience is the kind of listener said by Leonard Meyer to understand the *style* of the music listened to.[9]

9. Leonard Meyer, *Emotion and Meaning in Music* (Chicago: University of Chicago Press, 1956).

According to Meyer, listeners form *hypotheses*—expectations—on the basis of what they have heard so far, about what will happen next. These expectations are very weak indeed on the strength of merely a note or two but altogether stronger as the music plays on. Three types of musical "meanings" may be distinguished. There are *hypothetical* meanings, which are the musical events from among which the listener expects one to follow on what has been heard so far. There is *evident* meaning, which is the musical event that does in fact follow on what has been heard. And there is *determinate* meaning, which is the overall significance the listener can attach once the music is over, or is "timeless in memory,"[10] to the various perceived evident meanings in the piece, and perhaps to a number of the unrealized hypothetical meanings. The listener forms the expectations that constitute hypothetical meaning when the style in which the music is composed is understood. A style, for Meyer, is thus a system of probabilities of which the listener who grasps the style forms a more or less accurate estimate. To grasp a style is therefore to (be able to) have the kind of coherent musical experience that we have been talking about.

It is sometimes objected to Meyer's account that it must become redundant as soon as one is familiar with a work, for now one *knows* what's going to happen next, has no need for hypotheses, and is unlikely ever to be surprised (if one's memory is not defective).[11] But we can take heart from Michael Tanner, who quotes from chapter 11 of Thomas Love Peacock's *Headlong Hall:*

"I distinguish the picturesque and the beautiful, and I add to them, in the laying out of grounds, a third and distinct character, which I call *unexpectedness.*"

10. Ibid., pp. 37–38.

11. Indeed Meyer has worried about this himself. See his *Music, the Arts and Ideas* (Chicago: University of Chicago Press, 1969), pp. 46–52; and his article "On Rehearing Music," *Journal of the American Musicological Society* (1961): 257–67.

"Pray sir," said Mr. Milestone, "by what name do you distinguish this character, when a person walks round the grounds for the second time?"

"Anyone who has a rudimentary grasp of what art can achieve," says Tanner, "should regard with contempt [Mr. Milestone's] put-down, often quoted as final."[12] Now admittedly this is more of an admonition than an explanation; but only a few additional remarks are required to rebut Mr. Milestone more explicitly. The first thing to say, of course, is that the name by which the grounds' "third and distinct character" is distinguished a second time around is also "unexpectedness." For it is perfectly possible to know what is going to happen next and yet be surprised by it when it does. The reason for this is captured exactly in Hume's distinction between ideas and impressions, in which impressions are "those perceptions which enter with most force and violence," and ideas are "the faint images of these in thinking and reasoning": "The difference betwixt these consists in the degrees of force and liveliness, with which they strike upon the mind."[13] Thus the knowledge that such-and-such is about to happen (an idea) has a different character from the experience of that event when it does happen (the impression), for the idea lacks force and liveliness. And by the force and liveliness of an impression one can be surprised (or struck) even when one has the idea that the impression *will* be forceful and lively. Therefore, if something (a passage of music, for instance) has been found surprising the first time around, the certain prediction that it will recur when the music is listened to again—a prediction based upon the idea of an impression— need in no way prevent it from being found surprising when it does come to be experienced a second time; for the idea of an impression lacks certain of the characteristics (in our terms, the

12. Michael Tanner "Understanding Music," *Proceedings of the Aristotelian Society* (Supplementary vol., 1985): 222.
13. David Hume, *A Treatise of Human Nature*, p. 1.

perceptual properties) of the impression itself.[14] So I can be quite sure, for example, that I will find striking the glowingly garish colors of a painting by Odilon Redon without this giving me any reason not to go and see it again (in fact quite the reverse), or any reason not to *expect* to be surprised, when I do go again, by his glowingly garish colors.[15] These considerations, although allowing that someone might cease to be surprised at the surprising (through overexposure or boredom), are quite sufficient to deal with any objection of *this* kind to Leonard Meyer's position (or to the position I am advancing here).

According to Meyer, the kinds of musical event that form hypothetical and evident meanings, and that are later grasped in terms of determinate meaning, are the class of so-called purely musical events—those events which can be described in the specialist language of musical analysis. Listeners expect this note to follow rather than that; they expect a certain resolution to a chord progression; in a major-key sonata movement they expect the second subject to appear in the dominant; they expect a recapitulation of expository material after the development; they expect a longer or shorter coda that modulates more or less freely; and so forth. In addition, they may expect certain kinds of movement to follow the movement they are currently hearing—a rondo after the minuet, for instance, or a scherzo after the adagio. But if these listeners are not to weary of the piece, some of their expectations will be frustrated—by an unanticipated modulation, a false reprise, a slow finale or whatever. These "purely musical" events correspond to the varieties of perceptual property that we have been discussing. So in our present terms, we may say that Meyer's listener is the listener

14. It should be clear that this explanation does not depend upon the Humean theory of ideas. Hume's terminology just works rather neatly here.

15. Another way of making this point is suggested by Diana Raffman, who argues that our capacity for perceptual discrimination outstrips our capacity to recall or describe what we have perceptually discriminated. See her *Language, Music, and Mind* (Cambridge: MIT Press, 1993), chapters 5 and 6.

who forms expectations about the perceptual properties of an unfolding experience on the basis of the perceptual properties of the experience so far.

V

Meyer excludes expressive musical events from the class of "purely musical" events, believing the former to be by-products of the latter. A coherent musical understanding is, for him, "purely musical." There are several ways to arrive at this conclusion; and although Meyer's route is quite an individual one,[16] a general objection may be raised against any account which subordinates expressiveness in this way. This objection is simply that you cannot *entirely* grasp the "purely musical" *without* grasping the expressive; an attempt to make sense of a musical experience that has *only* "purely musical" perceptual properties will very frequently fail.[17] For example, and to put this in Meyer's terms, it is not true that the expectations conceived by the listener who grasps the probabilities constitutive of a given style are merely the "purely musical" ones. The understanding listener has expressive expectations too, which is why the apparently jolly main body of the finale of Mozart's G-minor String Quintet, K. 516, which follows three and a bit movements of dark, tragic music, is often felt to be an incoherent or incongruous element—and this in spite of its undoubted "purely musical" virtues. And its jollity is felt, by those who think this, to be a *musical* failing, an irrelevant intrusion. Expressive contrast, then, becomes a fact about structure. Consider also the common compositional practice of introducing a brand-new theme into a movement's coda. From a "purely musical" point of view this practice is quite hard to make sense of, for the new

16. For the annihilation of which, see Malcolm Budd, *Music and the Emotions* (London: Routledge and Kegan Paul, 1985), pp. 161–62.

17. This point receives some support from Peter Kivy's essay "A New Music Criticism?" in his collection *The Fine Art of Repetition* (Cambridge: Cambridge University Press, 1993).

theme may bear scant relation to any earlier material, and may seem to undermine the work's coherence; and when an attempt *is* made to justify a new theme on "purely musical" grounds, the results can appear strained and even comical (see, e.g., Wilfrid Mellers on the end of the *Appassionata*'s last movement[18]). Yet if you actually listen to, for example, the new theme in the coda of the finale of Mozart's Piano Concerto K. 453 there is nothing disturbing about it. For its expressiveness *is* related to the expressiveness of earlier material in the movement, as a kind of augmentation of exuberance—which listeners whose expectations are not confined to the "purely musical" will experience as the evident outcome of one of their most strongly held hypotheses, namely, that the movement will conclude exuberantly.

So the importance of expressive hypotheses for an account of musical understanding ought not to be overlooked. Indeed, we have now found a much better way than Busoni's to describe the intimate relation between feeling and style: perceptions of, and expectations about, one are integral to an understanding of the other. They cannot be thought of in mutual isolation. But these examples also show that there must be something in the experience of the listener whose musical experience is coherent other than "purely musical" perceptual properties; and the obvious suggestion is to say that that experience must have *expressive* perceptual properties also. Now we saw in Section II that perceptual properties combine with and modify one another. We would therefore expect expressive properties to combine with and modify "purely musical" properties. And they do, which we can perhaps show most clearly by considering performance.

The pianist Charles Rosen has written more strikingly than anyone about the "purely musical" significance of the B/B♭ conflict in Beethoven's *Hammerklavier* Sonata.[19] But very few (top-class) pianists can have played the crucial passages as though

18. Wilfrid Mellers, *Beethoven and the Voice of God* (London: Faber, 1983), pp. 106–7.
19. Charles Rosen, *The Classical Style* (London: Faber, 1971), pp. 413–20.

they mattered less. The shortfall in Rosen's playing is certainly not merely technical; and yet his performance suffers from an incohesiveness that makes a satisfying experience of it almost impossible to have. The reason seems to be that he overlooks the expressive aspect of the conflict, which *underlines* the "purely musical" structural point; so that in performance he weakens the structure. The expressive and the "purely musical" should *each* augment the structural considerations suggested by the other. Therefore a coherent experience of (a good performance of) Beethoven's sonata will have as one complex perceptual property a combination of expressive and "purely musical" aspects. And the *modification* of the "purely musical" by the expressive follows directly from this. For if it is possible to strengthen or, as Rosen does, to weaken the impact of "purely musical" factors in performance, then it is possible by the same token to strengthen or to weaken certain of Meyer's "purely musical" expectations. And if it is the case, as I have argued, that a listener who understands the music listened to also has expressive expectations about it, then it must also be the case that these may be strengthened or weakened in performance (as Rosen weakens them). The performer, then, is free within limits to augment or reduce some of the expectations of the listener who understands the music, and to do so by expressive means.

This point becomes especially clear if we consider the performance of musical excerpts—"bleeding chunks," as Tovey called them. For it follows that, within whatever are the appropriate limits, there will be ways of performing some excerpts so that the understanding listener will not conceive too many expectations which are thwarted; and that these ways will be expressive ways, which may well vary from whatever expressive practices would be appropriate if the excerpt were performed in context, where different expectations might be in order. Thus the modification of the "purely musical" by the expressive may function in certain cases as a clotting agent that, so to speak, prevents the significance of the excerpted chunk from bleeding away entirely and congeals it instead (perhaps into something different). So, for example, the way in which Siegmund's "Winterstürme" from *Die Walküre* should be performed as a concert excerpt (if it is going to be) will be different from the way it should be performed when it is heard as part of act 1. The song is quite sectional, and though in context this must be sufficiently apparent to mark the song off as an important, and quite unusual, "purely musical" event, it must not be emphasized so much that it breaks up the longer structure in which it appears. It seems that the best way of striking the balance is not to take the song too slowly, and to bring out the passionate, heroic elements of expression, so that expressively it matches its surroundings. In this manner the "purely musical" (potential) disruption is not underlined by a further marked expressive disruption. Done this way as an excerpt, however, it sounds rushed, loud and too short. It *sounds* like an excerpt from something, and its significance bleeds away; little of it congeals. But if the "purely musical" fact that the song is sectional is instead emphasized in performance—if it is taken more slowly and more strophically—and if expressive, tenderness is allowed to predominate and to underline this, then the song can just about stand by itself. Its significance congeals, and it no longer sounds like an excerpt. Yet this is just the manner of performance that causes maximum disruption if the song appears in its original context.

So performances of bleeding chunks present musical excerpts in such a way that their *original* significance cannot be understood. For of course by limiting the context within which the understanding listener forms expectations, the significance of an excerpt is not (exactly) the same as it would have been were it heard in its original surroundings. Thus I clearly cannot grasp the significance of Siegmund's "Winterstürme" as part of act 1 of *Die Walküre* if I hear it without the rest of act 1. But it certainly does not follow from this that I cannot understand it at all—that the practice of performing excerpts necessarily prevents me from understanding what I hear. For in the type of performance mentioned above, in which Siegmund's song is sung in a way that would be inappropriate if it formed part of a performance of act 1, I obviously can understand what I hear, for the manner of performance allows me to have a coherent experience of the song as I now hear it. The difference, of course, is that the significance I grasp in this experience is not the same as I would grasp in the experience of the song in a complete performance of *Die Walküre*. We can see, then, that by taking into account the modification of certain of the perceptual properties of a musical experience by others, we are given, among other things, a useful means for distinguishing between acceptable and unacceptable performances of excerpts. This feature of the present account appears to me to bode well for it: the capacity to explicate matters lying outside the immediate focus of concern, after all, is quite an encouraging feature for an account to have. So it is perhaps permissible to take our conclusions about bleeding chunks as a partial confirmation of the account of musical understanding upon which they depend: that to understand music is to be able to hear it in a certain way, is to have unfolding experiences that are coherent (i.e., that are, typically, in accord with whichever are the historically and culturally appropriate conventions for listening) to whatever extent the music, or the performance, permits; that among the perceptual properties of these experiences are the "purely musical" *and* the expressive (though properly, of course, *both* are musical: for both are properties of musical experiences, and some music cannot be understood *unless* the experience of it has expressive perceptual properties); and that these properties may combine with and modify one another in the ways that I have described, to yield unfolding experiences of great complexity and variety. Because expressive perceptual properties are properties or aspects of musical experience, moreover, the heresy of the *separable* experience ceases, in this context, to be an issue. The present characterization not only allows that an interest in passion may at the same time be an interest in the music to which it is related; it makes clear that an interest in at least some music is inadequate if it is not at the same time an interest in matters of passion.

CHAPTER FOUR

Musical Melisma

E pur si muove.
—Attributed to GALILEO GALILEI

We are now in a position to think rather more clearly about musical expressiveness, upon which all the relations between music and the passions that we are concerned with depend. Something is expressive of a passion if, first, by virtue of certain of its features it calls that passion to mind; and if, second, that passion does not need to be thought of as *someone's* passion. Thus the melancholy of which a weeping willow is expressive is not anybody's melancholy, and one need not mistakenly suppose that it is in order to identify the passion of which the willow is expressive. In Chapter 3 we saw that the experience of listening to music with understanding can be characterized as an experience having certain perceptual properties, some of which are expressive, some of which are rhythmic, and so on. It should now be clear that just as a rhythmic feature of a piece of music is any feature that may appropriately be the object of an experience having perceptual properties of rhythm, so an expressive feature of a piece of music is any feature that may appropriately be the object of an experience having perceptual properties of expressiveness. Therefore the attempt to understand musical expressiveness is, in part, the attempt to determine which features may be so experienced—to determine, in other words, which are the expressive features of music. That is the business of the present chapter.

I

The experience of harmony, timbre and tempo affect the experience of melodic pitch difference at the closing cadence of Sibelius's Seventh Symphony. That cadence has also a very strong character of finality (which would not be detected by Scruton's dove), which is produced largely by the interplay of harmony, tempo, rhythm and melody. Therefore the perceptual properties of certain quite complex experiences (properties of exaggerated pitch difference, and of finality) depend upon the combination of other perceptual properties; which is to say that they depend upon features of the music that are appropriately the objects of experiences already having those other perceptual properties—where "already," here, is to be understood as an indication of logical rather than chronological priority. When we ask which features of music are the expressive features, then, it is quite likely that the answer will be of the form "features already picked out as the objects of experiences having certain perceptual properties (such as harmony, tempo etc.)"; or more neatly, but elliptically, "features such as harmony, tempo etc." So it may be not only that in a complex musical experience expressiveness combines with and modifies "purely musical" features of the music (as we saw in the final section of the previous chapter) but also that it depends upon them.

Suppose, then, that the expressive features of music are (some set of) the "purely musical" ones. We must ask what it could possibly be in the "purely musical" that we recognize as expressive. Writing in 1601,[1] Jacopo Peri suggested that we recognize in the "purely musical" a resemblance to the expressive human voice: "In our speech some words are so intoned that harmony can be based on them. . . . Having in mind those inflections and accents that serve us in our grief, in our joy, and in similar states, I caused the bass to move in time to these, either more or

<hr>

1. Quoted in Oliver Strunk, *Source Readings in Music History* (New York: Norton, 1950), p. 374.

less, following the passions." And in similar vein, Thomas Reid thought an expressive melody was "an imitation of the tones of the human voice in the expression of some sentiment or passion."[2] Now it is clear that the claim made here is one about the portrayal or representation in music of the expressive human voice, and also that both writers take such portrayal to be intentional. It would therefore be a swift objection to this claim to point out that some composers of expressive music have *not* meant to imitate the expressive human voice (or even that they have deliberately avoided doing so)—an objection that, if successful, would show that the claim can suggest at best only a partial account of expressiveness in music (i.e., an account of only such expressive music as resembles, and was intended by its composer to resemble, the sound of the expressive human voice). But the substance of the claim can be retained even if explicit reference to intention is dropped. For if one thing resembles another thing sufficiently, then the first thing may put one in mind of the second regardless of whether it was meant to. But this relation of intended *or* unintended resemblance cannot uncontentiously be characterized as representation or portrayal, for many analyses of these concepts make intention central.[3] I shall therefore call the intention-neutral resemblance that music may bear to the human voice *melisma* (stretching, somewhat, one of the definitions of *melisma* offered in the *Oxford Companion to Music*[4]). So if we eliminate references to intention, the claim made by Peri and Reid can be stated as

2. In *Works of Thomas Reid,* ed. William Hamilton (Edinburgh: Longmans, Green, 1895), vol. 1, p. 504.

3. See, e.g., Roger Scruton, *Art and Imagination* (London: Methuen, 1974), p. 198; and Richard Wollheim, *Art and Its Objects,* 2d ed. (Cambridge: Cambridge University Press, 1980), pp. 206–7.

4. "The melisma is . . . often used merely for display purposes but also descriptively and for emotional expression (Handel, "Rejoice greatly" and "Thou shalt break them" in *Messiah;* Bach to such words as "wept" and "scourge" in his Passions)." In *Oxford Companion to Music,* ed. Percy Scholes (Oxford: Oxford University Press, 1970), p. 618.

follows: expressive music is music that, in virtue of its resemblance to the tones, inflections and accents of the expressive human voice, puts the listener in mind of such a voice. Expressive music bears a melismatic relation to the expressive human voice.

In trying to decide how adequate an account like this is, it will be useful first to locate those aspects of music which can call a voice to mind. Melody is the most obvious. We describe melodic lines as "sighing" and as "whispering," as "wailing," "shrieking" and "sobbing," as "hectoring," "declamatory," "wheedling" and "hysterical." In the majority of cases, where the description is apt, the contour of the melody (which is a function—partly—of its harmony) as well as its rhythm and timbre, will be melismatic. Timbre, by itself, may also have melismatic effect, in its resemblance to the thinner, sharper, richer, brighter, more honeyed or more shrill qualities of the expressive human voice. Throughout, aspects of the music are heard as having qualities audibly *in common* with vocal sounds. Shrillness is shrillness whether it emanates from a voice or from a wind quintet; and the timbre, contour and rhythm of a wheedling voice may (in principle) be equally the timbre, contour and rhythm of a melody. There is nothing metaphorical about these resemblances. If an expressive voice is, inter alia, shrill, then so—just as literally—may a musical timbre be shrill; and one resembles the other precisely inasmuch as two shrill sounds are alike. Kendall Walton is helpful here, when he says that "sounds are thought of as standing apart from their sources more easily than sights are, as objects of perception on their own, independent of the bells or trains or speech which might be heard by means of them. A sight is nearly always a sight *of* something, in our experience; a sound can be just a sound"[5]— which suggests that the comparison of sounds in respect of their

---

5. Kendall Walton, "What Is Abstract about the Art of Music?" *Journal of Aesthetics and Art Criticism* (1988): p. 352.

common qualities should be a very simple and direct comparison (and certainly more simple and direct than the comparison of sights), and thus that the shrillness, say, which two sounds share should be a point of similarity between them that is very easily discerned. So melisma ought to be rather striking, when the resemblance is close. And even when the resemblance is not that close the comparison facilitated by the "independence" of sounds should make melisma recognizable.

Suppose that a speaking voice is heard as sad in virtue of a combination of its features (such as its timbre, contour, rhythm and so on). To hear a voice as sad is therefore to be put in mind of sadness owing to the presence of those features. Music, too, can exhibit those features. On the present account, a piece of music is expressive of sadness if it has those features which are heard as sad when those features are the features of a voice. To hear music as expressive of sadness, then, is to be put in mind of a voice that is expressive of sadness, in virtue of those features that the voice and the music have in common. Of course, this states only what is *necessary.* Among the strange and striking noises that Berio directs the singers of *A-ronne* to produce, for example, are some that certainly put one in mind of the expressive human voice. Yet it is quite hard to hear the music as expressive—perhaps because a coherent experience does not require it. It is therefore insufficient that the music be heard merely to exhibit those features: the recognition of melisma requires that the hearer be *struck* by the resemblance, in virtue of those features, of music to voice. And this requirement appears to place something of a constraint upon the theory. For the expressive features of music will be heard as expressive *only* if they are relayed by the listener to the similar features of a voice; otherwise they will be heard merely as timbre, contour, rhythm and so on. According to Malcolm Budd, this constraint is too heavy for the theory to bear: "If the theory is understood to include the requirement that the listener should hear the music as resembling a sad voice in those respects which make the voice sad the theory has little attraction. . . . It is too strong: it is not necessary to realize which features a piece has in common with a sad voice if the music is to be heard as sad."[6] This objection, if good, would restrict the melisma theory to music that is *consciously* heard as voicelike, leaving all other expressive music to be explained in a different fashion. But the objection is not really compelling.

It is, of course, possible to find examples of melismatic music that is expressive in something like the required way. Some of the faster material in Brahms's Horn Trio, Op. 40, and especially in the finale, seems to exploit the conventionally expressive capabilities of the natural valveless horn, to convey the kind of rural jollity that goes with horses and copses and hedgerows; but at the climax of the much darker slow movement there is a sharply rising horn arpeggio that it is quite hard (for me, at least) not to hear as a cry of anguish—an utterly melismatic effect. Now it is true that I am conscious of the arpeggio as voicelike. But it is not clear to me that I "realize *which* features [the] piece of music has in common with [an anguished] voice" (my italics)—though I can hear that it does have features in common. If someone were to ask me why I heard the horn here as an anguished cry I would probably just sing the arpeggio to them; and in emphasizing, perhaps, the roughness of tone on the ascent, and the all but exhausted quality of it at the top, I suppose I would show in my singing that I did realize which at least some of the relevant features were. But if I were altogether hopeless at singing, and unable verbally to pick out the features I would emphasize if I *could* sing, I would have no means of showing that I realized which features those were; indeed, I would probably *not* realize which they were. And yet I could still quite easily hear the horn arpeggio as a cry of anguish. Therefore it is not necessary in any strong sense to "realize which

6. Malcolm Budd, *Music and the Emotions* (London: Routledge and Kegan Paul, 1985), p. 143.

features a piece of music has in common with [an anguished] voice if the music is to be heard as [anguished]." What is necessary, on the melisma theory, is only that the resemblance of music to voice that strikes the listener can in principle be *explained* by reference to the features that music and voice have in common; it is not necessary that the listener can (or does) do this when listening to the music (and nor is it necessary that the listener can, or does, do this at any other time).

But we can go further. For it is not even clear that the idea of an anguished *voice* need be present to the listener who hears Brahms's arpeggio as expressive of anguish. I have said that the listener is "struck" by the resemblance of music to voice, that this resemblance "puts the listener in mind of" a voice; and Budd's objection suggested that this "striking" and "being put in mind of" would have to go on at an explicit, conscious level. But with the weakening of that objection it is now possible to suppose that the perception of resemblance may sometimes happen at a level of which the listener is *not* conscious, so that the listener thinks Brahms's arpeggio expressive of anguish but does not think consciously of an anguished voice. Such a listener hears as expressive those features of the music which unconsciously strike him or her as resembling features of an expressive human voice—and, although the listener is unaware of this, the expressiveness that is heard is melismatic. Now, the idea of such a listener is perfectly plausible, for comparable instances of being unconsciously struck by resemblances are commonplace. I doubt, for example, whether many people think explicitly of an alternately rumbling and explosive voice when they think of thunder as "angry," nor of a thin and wailing voice when they hear the wind as "desolate." Yet it is difficult to suppose that at least some such connections are not being made—melismatic connections, which may, of course, be explicit in the experience of some listeners—when thunder or wind are heard in this way. I would guess that the reason why such connections may be made unconsciously has less to do with any merely conventional association (e.g., the *habit* of thinking of thunder as "angry") than with the ubiquity and importance in our lives of the expressive human voice. Its tones, inflections and accents affect us intimately and directly; and to these qualities of sound it would be surprising if we had failed to become sensitive. And to the extent that this would be surprising, it would be surprising if we were not to move easily (and perhaps unconsciously) from the perception of those qualities of sound to the thought of the state of which those qualities of sound are, in their primary context, expressive, even when the sound having those qualities is not the human voice but is instead a piece of music, or some weather. I suggested earlier that similarities of sound quality should be very easily discerned, and so that melisma ought to be striking. If the considerations I have just offered are persuasive, we can now say that melisma may be so *immediately* striking that it isn't noticed at all—which isn't the paradox that it sounds.

It is of course true that the introduction into an explanation of unconscious processes is usually better avoided, but it may sometimes be appropriate; and when, as here, those processes can in principle be made quite explicit, such an explanation need occasion no alarm at all. If it proves to be impossible to identify which features a particular piece of music shares with an expressive human voice, then it cannot be assumed to share any, and no amount of gesturing toward the unconscious will alter this. So the present style of explanation admits as melismatic *no* music that cannot in principle be experienced, consciously and explicitly, as resembling the human voice in whichever are the relevant ways. It merely allows that some such music may also be heard as expressive by listeners who are unaware of the melisma that underpins their experience. This means that it need not always be *obvious* whether a particular piece of expressive music is melismatically expressive.

A melisma theory of expressiveness, then, has its attractions; indeed, I believe that melisma plays a quite pervasive part in much of our musical experience. But certainly such a theory is limited. The expressiveness of many musical works cannot be explained in terms of resemblance to the expressive human voice, whether consciously perceived or not. The opening piano chord, and the first low F, of Rachmaninoff's Second Piano Concerto set a darkly expressive scene; and yet I cannot conceive of a plausible melismatic explanation for the effect. The timbre of the chord bears no relation that I can hear to any voice, nor does the drop to the bass note suggest the contour of any expressive utterance. There seem to be no melismatic resemblances here to be made explicit. And the inadequacy of the theory as a total explanation becomes more marked, if anything, when we turn to expressive vocal music, for which it might have been expected to account most easily. Of course, the presence of a singing voice does increase the incidence of melisma. But no human voice ever expressed itself in the shapes that Webern wrote (in, e.g., the songs with E♭ clarinet and guitar); and if we strip away everything melismatic—and there's a lot—from Tristan's delirium (*Tristan*, act 3, scene 1), we are left with pages of painfully wrought expressive music that owe nothing discernible, for their expressiveness, to the extramusical habits of the human voice. So however convincing the melisma theory may be in explaining the expressiveness of some music (which is to say, very convincing) the burden of explaining all musical expressiveness is certainly too heavy for it.

II

We must look for other potentially expressive features of music, then—or, more accurately, for other (nonvocal) respects in which "purely musical" features such as melody, rhythm, and so on, may be heard as expressive. Musical *motion* seems a powerful candidate here, and its candidacy has a long pedigree.

> Ever since antiquity . . . it was the concept of motion that provided a connection between music and affection . . . ; both

musical and psychic motions are subject to the same laws. . . .
The movements of the animal spirits, according to Nicola Vin-
centino (1555) and Gioseffo Zarlino (1558), are the reason for the
effects of intervals: major "stretched" intervals of the second,
third, and sixth attune to joy, while minor "contracted" intervals on the contrary attune to sadness. "What is passionate in
us," wrote Herder concerning the effects of music, "rises and
falls, leaps or creeps, and slowly paces. Now it becomes urgent,
now hesitant, now stirred more feebly, now more strongly."[7]

Thus music is conceived as sharing properties of motion with
the (very Cartesian) human soul. Sometimes the thought is that
music's motions set in train similar motions in the listener's
"animal spirits," thereby causing him or her to experience some
passion of which the music is then said to be expressive;[8] and
sometimes the thought is that in sharing some particular quality of motion with the "animal spirits" the music represents or
portrays a passion, of which it is then said to be expressive and
which the listener recognizes without necessarily coming to feel
anything.[9] In this chapter it is the second of these possibilities
that is of interest to us. The first possibility, quite apart from its
dependence upon a doubtful philosophy of mind, is primarily
about what I have called sympathetic response, which we are
not yet ready to deal with. The second possibility speaks primarily about the recognition of musically expressive qualities,
through their resemblance to certain of the qualities of affective
experience, and is thus very much to the point.

In our discussion of this second possibility there are two
things that we can say straight away: first, that the resemblance
here posited need not be one intended by the composer (for the

7. Carl Dahlhaus, *Esthetics of Music* (Cambridge: Cambridge University Press,
1982), p. 19.
8. See, e.g., Daniel Webb, *Observations on the Correspondence between Poetry
and Music* (London, 1769), pp. 4–10.
9. See, e.g., Charles Batteux, writing in 1746, quoted in Peter le Huray and
James Day, eds., *Music and Aesthetics in the Eighteenth and Early Nineteenth
Centuries* (Cambridge: Cambridge University Press, 1988), pp. 38–44.

same reasons that the resemblance underpinning vocal melisma need not be intended); and second, that much depends upon the satisfactory solution of two difficulties associated with the idea of "musical motion." These difficulties can be swiftly stated. For there to be motion, there must be a space in which the motion happens; yet music is not a spatial phenomenon. And there must be something that moves; yet nothing moves when one pitch is followed by another. So because nothing in music seems to satisfy either requirement, there would seem to be nothing that could count as musical motion.

Now of course it is true that many of our most common locutions when we speak about music do seem to refer to a species of musical space (and to movement within it). Indeed, the categories of space and motion appear to be quite basic to our musical experience. We speak of notes as being more or less distant from one another and as being higher or lower; but clearly we cannot be referring to any real physical space in which these notes are, literally, positioned. The top and bottom notes of a wind instrument proceed from exactly the same place (the end of the tube), and at no point do they occupy locations distinct from one another. So difference in pitch cannot literally mean difference in spatial position. But suppose instead that the musical "space" in which pitches occupy higher or lower positions is simply a very good *analogy* of physical space, so that changes of position in musical space provide a very good analogy for changes of position in physical space—that is, for motion. Peter Kivy has something of this sort in mind when he says that "the rise in pitch, both in natural organisms and machines, betokens a rise in energy level. The faster the wings beat, the shriller the sound; likewise, the more energy expended, the higher the engine's whine." The connection between pitch and space, and between space and motion, depends upon "the intimate relation of pitch to energy, and energy to motion."[10]

10. Peter Kivy, *The Corded Shell* (Princeton: Princeton University Press, 1980), p. 55.

Similarly, Wilson Coker states that "to move in a given direction from a fixed pitch by a large interval normally is to use more energy for that pitch displacement than is required to move in the same direction from that pitch by a smaller interval."[11] In both cases, pitch (or pitch difference) is correlated with energy (or energy difference); and energy levels are then interpreted as the analogues of levels (i.e., elevations) of physical position. A high note, then, occupies a position (relative to energy) analogous to the position (relative to physical space) occupied by the top of something tall—which is to say, a high position.

But this attempt to ground an analogy between position in musical "space" and position in physical space fails for two reasons. The first is that the correlation between pitch and energy cannot be made good. It is true that high sounds are of high frequency; but it is not true that a sound of high frequency somehow possesses more energy than a sound of low frequency, for in this context energy is a matter of intensity (i.e., of volume). It is true that the amount of waste energy dissipated as noise when energy is injected into an inefficient system (like an engine) increases as the amount of energy injected is increased. But it is not necessarily true that the pitch of the resultant noise is higher as the amount of energy injected or dissipated is higher (which is why you can turn your stereo up without raising the pitch of your music). And when it *is* true that the pitch of the noise is higher (as with a jet engine), it is not true that the noise presents itself, in any phenomenological way, as somehow more "energetic" than a noise of lower pitch, but of equal volume, dissipated by another inefficient system. Further—and this time against Coker—it is true sometimes (to say "normally" would be to say too much) that "to move in a given direction from a fixed pitch by a large interval . . . is to use more energy . . . than is required to move in the same direction from that pitch by a smaller interval"; but this is true only when the "fixed pitch" is

<hr />

11. Wilson Coker, *Music and Meaning* (New York: Free Press, 1972), p. 43.

roughly in the middle of the pitch range possible for whatever it is that is producing the sound. If you sing the lowest note you can, it will cost you much less effort to sing next a significantly higher note than an insignificantly higher note; and the same goes, mutatis mutandis, when the "fixed pitch" from which you start is the highest note that you can sing. So the correlation between pitch and energy level (or between pitch difference and energy difference) is quite inadequate to ground an analogy between position in musical "space" and position in physical space.

But even if pitch and energy levels *were* directly proportional, the choice of energy levels as a helpful correlative of pitch would still be significantly wrong. For differences in energy levels consist in there being more or less of something present—that is, of energy. Differences of pitch, on the other hand, are not experienced as differences in the degree to which anything is present: there is nothing that a high note is heard as having more of than a low note, or anything, except pitch, that is heard to increase as pitch is increased. As Edmund Gurney points out, "Differences of pitch . . . are neither differences of *kind,* as between red and blue colours, or between bitter and sweet tastes, or between a violin-note and a clarionet-note; nor differences of *strength* or *degree of intensity,* as between bright and moderate light, or between very sweet and slightly sweet tastes, or between a loud note and a soft note; but they are differences of *distance and direction,* clearly and indisputably."[12] Thus, the choice of a dimension involving differences in degree (like energy) as the dimension along which musical pitches have their positions, so that they have positions analogous to positions in physical space, is inapt. And Gurney is surely right to distinguish pitch differences instead as differences of distance and direction. A pitch may be more or less close to another pitch; and a pitch that is lower than a given pitch is heard as distant from it in an opposite direction to that in which a pitch higher than the given pitch is heard as distant from it. It is in just this way that the range of pitches has orientation for us, and it is in just this way that such a range is more closely analogous to a range of positions in physical space than either range is analogous to a set of values along a dimension of degree (such as energy); for different points along a straight line in physical space are also distinguished by differences of distance and direction, and by nothing else.

So the establishment of *orientation* in the pitch range requires no appeal to any further value, which allows the analogy between pitch orientation and orientation in physical space to be drawn directly. But of course this gets us only so far. For the species of orientation established is unspecific, having no more the character of up-to-down than it has of left-to-right. So although "high" notes and "low" notes are distinguished, they are not necessarily distinguished as high or low (any more than they are necessarily distinguished as left or right). Is there, then, any way to show that the orientation of pitches *must* be analogous to the orientation of points on a vertical line, as the Western experience of music appears to assume? I think that probably there isn't—although suggestions can be made. It might be argued, for instance, that up and down *in general* play a more significant or basic part in our perceptual experience than left and right do; and so that we tend, in structuring our thoughts about the perceptual experience of phenomena without either dimension, to prefer vertical schemata to horizontal ones—on account of which it would not be surprising that we think of pitch in the terms we do. But I don't know how the priority of the vertical in our perceptual experience could possibly be demonstrated; and even if it could be demonstrated, and even if this were accepted as the explanation of our vertical orientation of pitch, it would still provide no reason for us to regard as "high" the end of the pitch range that we do think high. The range could just as easily have been oriented the other way up.

A more direct and promising suggestion, however, derives from Carroll Pratt. He thinks that "in addition to the purely qualitative pitch-character by which tones are readily placed with respect to one another along a scale there may be discovered an intrinsic spatial character in tones," which derives from the fact that although high tones do not literally proceed from a higher position in space than low tones, at any rate they *sound* as if they do.[13] If this is so, then both the vertical orientation of the pitch range and the particular way up that range is oriented, would make sense. But is it true that high tones sound as if they come from higher positions than low tones? I think it is, to an extent; but it is of course difficult to know whether this phenomenological fact explains, or is explained by, our tendency to think of high notes as "high." To settle this we would have to see if some reason could be given why high notes should sound as if they come from higher, which makes no appeal to any independent tendency that we might have to think of them as higher anyway. I offer the following suggestion tentatively. Loud bass notes make the floor shake in a way that loud treble notes don't. This is because the dimensions of a floor (several meters) are of the same order of magnitude as the wavelength of some sounds of a low pitch, and structures of a given size resonate when struck by sounds of a comparable wavelength (which is why you need a high noise, with a wavelength of only a few centimeters, to smash a glass). Now it is true that the walls and ceilings of a room may also resonate at these frequencies (though very little else will: most rooms don't contain a lot of things that are several meters across); but we are not usually in physical contact with walls and ceilings as we are with floors; and floors of course are beneath us. So perhaps bass notes sound as if they come from a lower position because something associated with them (i.e., vibration), and of which we are often aware, literally does come from a lower position (i.e., from the

13. Carroll Pratt, *The Meaning of Music* (New York: McGraw-Hill, 1931), p. 54, for a penetrating discussion of which see Budd, *Music and the Emotions,* chapter 3.

floor beneath our feet, or beneath our chair). Naturally this would mean that if our aural experience were somewhat different, in that most or all of it took place while we were strapped to the ceiling, we would say that those notes we now call "low" were "high" (i.e., were associated with vibration often felt from above us). This suggestion may be rather inelegant, but it isn't especially implausible; and it does provide at least a partial reason why—as floor-dwellers—we orient the pitch range the way we do.

But be this as it may, it is certainly the case that we do orient the pitch range vertically and that we do agree which pitches are to be called "higher" and which "lower." Perhaps (although I doubt it) "higher" and "lower" will in the end turn out to be just arbitrary names for the directions within this range. The analogies between musical "space" (and pitch positions within it) and physical space (and point positions within that) will then remain incomplete and unsusceptible to further substantive elaboration. But there are independent reasons to suppose that this outcome is likely in any case; for pitch positions and point positions are quite dissimilar. It is—to give just one example—part of the concept of a position in physical space that two physical objects can't be in it at once; yet it seems not to be true that two musical objects cannot simultaneously occupy a pitch position—as when a trumpet and a piano sound the same note. The two sounds are heard as being in the same musical position and yet are heard as two distinct sounds.[14] But the incompleteness of these analogies need not worry us very greatly. For I believe that a range of pitch differences—which have properties of distance and direction—will prove to be sufficiently and literally spacelike for our present purposes. The description of differences of direction within this range as "up" and "down" is perhaps not literal; although if Pratt is right, then

14. As others have pointed out: see, e.g., Budd's *Music and the Emotions,* p. 180; or Roger Scruton's *The Aesthetic Understanding* (London: Methuen, 1983), p. 83.

that description *is* literally true of the way these differences *sound*—which is all that actually matters. But certainly much of our musical experience depends upon our experiencing pitch difference under the descriptions "up" and "down," whether or not these descriptions are literal. To imagine musical experience otherwise "is to imagine a thorough-going alteration" of it—"musically speaking, the greatest difference imaginable."[15]

So let us take the oriented pitch range to be the musical analogue of space. We now have a dimension within which (some analogue of) motion might happen—that is, within which there may, along a second, temporal (and musically unproblematic) axis, be events of a certain kind. But for there to be motion there must also be something that moves. Yet when one note follows another it seems that there is *nothing* that moves, for one pitch is simply displaced by a different pitch, to give a bare succession—and not movement. Consider a siren, however, or a string portamento: of these we can surely say that there is something that "goes (moves) up and down"—so that there is a thing (the sound made by the siren or the string) which changes position relative to the oriented pitch range. Inasmuch, then, that a continuously identifiable thing which occupies successively different positions is moving, the sounds made by the siren and the string are in motion, quite literally (and quite independently of whether the orientation of the pitch range is up-down, left-right or whatever). But of course the siren and the portamento occupy not only successively different positions in the pitch range but also *all intervening* positions (as moving objects do in physical space)—which is one reason why those sounds are the continuously identifiable individuals that we experience as being, unproblematically, in motion. But sirens and portamenti are not in this regard representative of musical sounds in general. The sounds made by the other kind of siren (the old police one), by nonscooping strings, by wind instruments and by

15. Scruton, *The Aesthetic Understanding*, pp. 80–81.

pianos do not, when changing pitch, successively occupy all the positions between pitches: the next pitch simply supersedes the last. It is this difference which is often felt to be crucial.[16]

But how crucial is it? What is under threat, of course, is the satisfaction of the requirement that there be some "continuously identifiable individual" that can be said to move. The sound of a siren satisfies this condition (in one way) because the path of its motion is unbroken. A rise of a fifth on the oboe, by contrast, seems not to: there are two successive oboe sounds, pitched a fifth apart. And yet we *do* speak of the sound of an oboe "going" up and down. This fact is certainly not to be explained by appeal to a perceptual illusion (analogous to the illusion of movement produced by film—and indeed to that produced by the digital recording of a siren) in which we mistake a succession of differently pitched discrete sounds for a sirenlike scoop between them.[17] For the continuously identifiable individual that moves is not an illusory construct. When we hear an oboe scale as an ascending movement we do not, mistakenly or otherwise, experience the scale as if it were a scoop (unless the scale is *extremely* fast—in which case there *is* a kind of illusion); we experience movement in a succession of pitched sounds. A better suggestion, for the simple sort of case we are considering (more complex cases will be mentioned presently), is that the experiential analogue of an individual that is continuously identifiable through pitch change is the sound of the instrument whose pitch changes. We can identify the sound of an oboe quite easily, and have little trouble saying whether it is an oboe or another instrument that is responsible for a particular sound. We achieve this identification, in our experience of the sound, by means of the perceptual property of *timbre* that our experience of the sound has. Therefore if an

16. By, e.g., Budd, *Music and the Emotions*, p. 44; Scruton, *The Aesthetic Understanding*, p. 80; and Dahlhaus, *Esthetics of Music*, p. 84.

17. Cf. Budd, *Music and the Emotions*, p. 44.

oboe sounds one pitch and then another immediately after, we hear a continuously identifiable sound (that of an oboe) that occupies successively different positions relative to the pitch range—which is to say that we experience the oboe sound as *moving.* The oboe sound does not move through all the intervening pitch positions, of course, but this seems not to be crucial; for that is just the difference between an oboe and a siren.

The species of movement that features as a perceptual property of the oboe sound, then, is obviously dissimilar to physical movement in some respects (e.g., in continuity of positional change); but it is neither a particularly obscure species nor a very rare one. We attribute movement to prices, for instance (or, more strictly, to commodities relative to a price range). But if bacon "goes up" overnight from $.95 to $.97 we don't suppose that at some point (dawn, perhaps?) it must have cost $.96; for that is not how price differences work. Still less do we suppose that a rise of one cent (analogous to a rise in pitch to the next adjacent note) must involve the bacon at some point costing $.95729; for that price doesn't fit in with our currency arrangements (with our pitch arrangements). The fact is that, first, we are inclined to speak of movement wherever we detect something continuously identifiable (like a commodity or a sound) occupying successively different positions relative to a dimension (like a price range or a pitch range); and that, second, physical movement, such as that of a bullet occupying successively different positions relative to a firing range, involves in addition something that commodity and sound movements do not—that is, continuity of positional change.

Now of course the requirement that movement between positions must also be movement through all intervening positions pervades our experience of objects in physical space. That musical movement (among other kinds) often violates this requirement reflects the different relations that hold between musical objects (like oboe sounds) and the oriented pitch range (a difference already encountered above, when we saw that two sounds could be in the same pitch position at once). The essence of the difference seems to be that we find it harder to abstract the idea of a physical object from the idea of a physical continuum than we do to abstract the idea of a musical object (or a commodity) from the idea of a musical continuum (or a price continuum). If we find that a physical object has moved to somewhere it wasn't before, we infer that in the meantime it has passed through places in between: and often we make the truth of this inference a condition of the object's identity. But we do not make this inference of, nor (as we have seen) do we impose this condition upon, musical (and other) objects we deem to have moved (and in fact neither any longer are such demands made of *physical* objects by those most closely interested in them: for electrons are said to move from one quantum state to another without passing through any intervening state). This suggests that *identity* through positional change is more basic to the concept of movement than is *continuity* of positional change, and that continuity of positional change is not basic even to the concept of identity (within a dimension).

So, at a rudimentary level, we may say of musical movement that the individual experienced as moving is the sound of a musical instrument, which is distinguished by its timbre; and that *where* it moves is within the (literally) spacelike dimension of the pitch range. (The preference for a coherent musical experience, however, is likely to limit the number of cases in which movement is actually heard. In most cases, for instance, a bare change in pitch, if the first pitch is widely separated in time from the second, is unlikely to be experienced as a movement by the listener who understands what he is hearing). If the up-down orientation of that range *is* arbitrary, then so to a degree are the kinds of movements that we hear: perhaps they might as easily have been lateral movements (though movements none-theless). It is clear, too, because this kind of musical movement is distinguished by timbre, and because timbre is a perceptual property of the experience of musical sounds, that such musical movement must also be a perceptual property of that experience. But of course it is a more complex perceptual property than this rudimentary description can capture. For when we hear musical movement we often hear as moving not a single instrumental sound, but a collection of such sounds, consecutively or simultaneously. We can hear, for example, as a single movement a melodic line whose successive pitches are allotted to a series of different instruments, and which is accompanied by the motions of still other instruments. This is a sophisticated form of listening; indeed in some very complicated music, such as Webern's, the principal line, or *Hauptstimme,* which is shared by many instruments, is marked as such in the score so that it may be played in a way that allows it to be heard. This sophisticated (but not uncommon) form of listening should prompt us to revise the emphasis given so far to individual instrumental sounds. It seems that the emphasis ought instead to be laid upon the musical *patterns,* such as melodies, where musical movement is actually heard. In certain melodies, which have been arranged very simply so that the principal line is given to just one solo instrument, "instrumental sound" will certainly count as an individual that, in these particular patterns, may be heard as moving. There will be no difference in such cases between hearing the movement of the instrumental sound and hearing the movement of the melody. But where the music is more complex, or where it has been arranged in a more complicated way, the melody heard as moving will often not be coextensive or interchangeable with any individual instrumental sound. It will be in the patterned relationships constituting the melody itself that motion is heard— rather as the crest of a wave is seen to travel horizontally, even though the individual drops of water that the wave pattern comprises undergo no horizontal displacement. Or perhaps we might think of this more complex kind of movement as a species of relay running, in which we are able to distinguish the individual runners (the particular instrumental sounds) from the baton (the melodic line) which they pass between them. The listener whose experience of music is coherent is able to follow and distinguish between melodic lines (batons) and also to assign to them different degrees of significance. So to understand the melodic lines of a musical work is, according to this line of thought, to be able to hear in certain ways the various movements that it comprises.

This now brings us to a point where we can make some sense of the suggestion aired at the beginning of this section—that music can be heard as expressive in virtue of the resemblance it bears to the motions characteristic of certain forms of passionate experience. Some substance has been given to the initially opaque notion of musical movement upon which this suggestion depends; and the way might thus seem open to appeal to some second kind of melisma—a movement-based melisma— to supplement the vocal melisma explored in Section I. Between them it is possible that they might account for the experience of music as expressive. Whether this is so, and what exactly a "movement-based melisma" might be, are the questions that will occupy us in the next chapter.

CHAPTER FIVE

Melisma Assessed

The earth sings MI, FA, MI so that you may infer even from
the syllables that in this our domicile MIsery and FAmine
obtain.

—JOHANN KEPLER, *Harmonices Mundi.*

We saw in the preceding chapter that vocal melisma might,
within quite narrow limits, function unproblematically as a
resource for musical expressiveness. And the suggestion that a
second kind of melisma—a movement-based or *dynamic* kind—
might also be possible received some support from the analysis
given in Section II of musical space and musical movement. But
we are not yet in a position to take those latter findings for
granted. Vocal melisma, remember, was shown to resemble
expressive human utterance in a quite literal way, so that its
capacity to function in an account of expressiveness in music
was established directly. Musical movement, by contrast, appeared to be less obviously literal; so there is still reason to
doubt whether an account of expressiveness that incorporates
it, as the basis for a dynamic form of melisma, will be an
adequate one. The fact that musical movement diverges, then,
with respect to continuity of positional change, from our ordinary experience of physical movement prompts the question
whether it is *literally* true of our musical experience that it has
the perceptual property of movement.

I

Gurney called musical movement "Ideal movement," and Scruton describes it as an "ineliminable metaphor"—a usage, incidentally, exploded by Malcolm Budd.[1] But I believe I have done enough in the previous chapter to suggest that such grand and dark sayings represent an overreaction (the "Ideal movement" of bacon prices would also be "ineliminably metaphorical" on these constructions). For the difference between musical (and other) movement as I have described it and physical movement is not great; and if we *do* agree in the end to call musical movement metaphorical, then we should bear in mind how limited is the nature of the metaphor we employ. Budd says that "unless the underlying point of a metaphor is understood its characterization as a metaphor is unrevealing."[2] And here the "underlying point" is quite clear: it is to bring under a single concept phenomena whose similarities are far more significant than their differences. We call "movement" a phenomenon that is exactly like the phenomenon usually called "movement," except with respect to one characteristic. But that characteristic, I have argued, is of only superficial significance, and is perhaps not even possessed by every instance of *physical* movement. "A dead metaphor," according to William Charlton, "is an expression used in an extended sense in which it does, in fact, apply, while a living metaphor is an expression used in a sense in which the user knows it to be inapplicable, for the purpose of securing an aesthetic advantage. . . . As soon as a word has a metaphorical sense in which it applies to a thing, its application to that thing ceases to be a living and becomes a dead metaphor. . . . A metaphorical sense is a sense in which the semantics

1. Edmund Gurney, *The Power of Sound* (London: Smith, Elser, 1880), p. 85; Roger Scruton, *The Aesthetic Understanding* (London; Methuen, 1983), p. 85; and Malcolm Budd, "Understanding Music," *Proceedings of the Aristotelian Society* (Supplementary vol., 1985): 239–45.

2. Malcolm Budd, *Music and the Emotions* (London: Routledge and Kegan Paul, 1985), p. 45.

of a language permits us to use a word."[3] "Musical movement," then, if the expression is metaphorical, is a very dead metaphor indeed, which—so thoroughly unadventurous is it—it is hard to imagine as ever having led a vigorous life.

There is good reason, therefore, to regard talk of "musical movement" as being figurative only to the extent that a very dead metaphor is figurative—which is to say, hardly figurative at all. But it will be helpful if we can devise a measure of metaphor-death for use, as it were, in the field; for some of our more elaborate descriptions of musical movement may involve factors not adequately covered by the characterization of "musical movement" offered in Chapter 4; and these would serve considerably to complicate the task in hand. The kind of measure we need can be derived from the following vintage piece of Fowler: a dead metaphor is

> sometimes liable, under the stimulus of an affinity or a repulsion, to galvanic stirrings indistinguishable from life . . . ; in *the sifting of evidence,* the metaphor is so familiar that it is about equal chances whether *sifting* or *examination* will be used, & that a sieve is not present to the thought—unless indeed someone conjures it up by saying *All the evidence must first be sifted with acid tests,* or *with the microscope*—; under such a stimulus our metaphor turns out to have been not dead but dormant; . . . the Latin *examino* . . . meant originally to weigh; but, though weighing is not done with acid tests or microscopes any more than sifting, *examine* gives no convulsive twitches, like *sift,* at finding itself in their company; *examine,* then, is . . . stone-dead metaphor, . . . & *sift* only half dead, or three-quarters.[4]

Thus a metaphor is dead to the extent that it fails to twitch when used, in its metaphorical context, as if it were a literal expres-

3. William Charlton, "Living and Dead Metaphors," *British Journal of Aesthetics* (1975): 174–78.
4. Henry Watson Fowler, *Modern English Usage* (Oxford: Oxford University Press, 1965), p. 359.

sion. If "sift" literally did mean "assess" it wouldn't stir at all (it wouldn't be a metaphor). But also, to the extent that a metaphor fails to twitch, in its metaphorical context, when confronted with adjectives and adverbial expressions from its *literal* context, it is also dead. "Sifting the evidence *finely*," for instance, creates no disturbance—the half-dead metaphor is extended without resurrection. "Sifting the evidence *with a rhythmic jiggle*," on the other hand, extends and revivifies the metaphor considerably. If the metaphor virtually never twitches under the second condition, then not only is it very dead but its metaphorical use must be so minimally removed from its literal use as scarcely to be metaphorical at all. The considerations offered in the preceding chapter suggest that this will turn out to be true of the dead-metaphor "musical movement."

Things that move physically can move "jerkily," "smoothly," "agitatedly," "restlessly," "galumphingly," "bouncily," "stodgily," "soaringly" and so forth. These are adverbial expressions from the literal context of "movement" (which is not, of course, to say that they are all *literal* expressions from that context); and it is clear that they provoke no "galvanic stirrings" from "musical movement" when made to qualify it. Music can move "jerkily," "smoothly," "bouncily," "stodgily" and so forth every bit as well as a stoat or a heart muscle can (indeed it seems more versatile— without disaster—than either); and just as we can say (elliptically) of a stoat that it is "bouncy," or of a heart muscle that it is "agitated," so we can describe music as "jerky," "smooth," "restless" or "stodgy," without a twitch. But we *cannot* say of music (as we could, obscurely or falsely, say of a stoat) that its movement is "supersonic," for music's movement is not of *that* kind, and the metaphor springs meaninglessly to life. We will probably not want to say of music that its movement is "motorized," because to do so would be to be either impenetrable or mistaken (as it would be to say the same of a stoat); and we should be chary of describing music's movements as "flapping," for such a description is unlikely to fit well the movements of many pieces of music (or of many stoats, for that matter). It is only the first kind of use that enlivens the metaphor; merely obscure, mistaken or improbable uses leave the metaphor moribund and draw notice instead to the doubtful intentions of the speaker. As a rule, the straightforward cases (i.e., those that are not obscure, mistaken, improbable or disturbing to the metaphor) are those in which a property attributed to music is neither a quantity (like miles per hour) nor a defining quality of the motion of some very special class of mover (like a motorized mover). Yet, of course, even in these straightforward cases, if it is not true of music that it literally "moves" then it cannot be literally true of it that it "moves jerkily," either (however dead the metaphor of movement). But in saying that music "moves jerkily" we are not introducing a new metaphor: we are only extending a dead one; and it is *within the scope* of the dead metaphor that these extensions can make—literally—true or false statements. Therefore, inasmuch as we may speak properly of musical movement, we may, by the same token, speak truly or falsely of "jerky," "galumphing" and "restless" musical movement; for in admitting these adjectives we admit nothing but the movement itself.

II

From this position it is quite easy to see how music may be related to a number of psychological states without the introduction of any further mechanism. For many of the adjectives of musical movement apply also to the bodily movements of human beings. Thus music may share with the bodies of human beings certain qualities of motion. But the names of some of those qualities of motion are also the names of psychological states, or passions, which have those qualities as their defining features; so that a person in such a state experiences movements in and of his body that have those qualities. A "jaunty" person moves, and feels himself to move, jauntily; a "calm" person moves, and feels himself to move, calmly. "Jauntiness" and "calm" are the names of qualities of movement that define the behavior and experience of someone in the relevant co-nominal psychological state. Therefore, "in so far as similar forms of movement may be presented tonally, the same words apply equally well to musical effects"; and hence Pratt's famous dictum that musical characteristics "*sound the way moods feel.*"[5] The claim here is not that because music may move jauntily it may somehow partake of or exemplify the psychological state of jauntiness. The claim is quite simply that a certain word— *jaunty*—may be applied with equal propriety both to a psychological state and to a kind of movement that gives its name to that state (a movement that music may partake of or exemplify). Therefore "jaunty" music is not so much *expressive* of jauntiness as simply, itself, jaunty, so that it is related to its co-nominal state by resembling it (in its defining respect). But it is clear that the number of psychological states or passions to which music may be so related is small, for most psychological states are neither named after qualities of motion nor defined in terms of them;[6] and it is clear, too, that the relation in question must be significantly dependent upon language: for it is only with respect to a language that names *some* psychological states after qualities of motion that such a relation can obtain at all. Pratt thinks that music's capacity to "sound the way moods feel"—in the sense described—accounts for a true description of the prelude to *Tristan* as "ardent, erotic, full of suspense, longing, unfulfillment."[7] But, as Budd remarks, "When we experience a passionate erotic desire that is uncertain of fulfillment our condition does not derive its name from the kinds of bodily motion that we may feel when in that condition."[8] So the degree to which the description of music in psychological terms can be

5. Carroll Pratt, *The Meaning of Music* (New York: McGraw-Hill, 1931), p. 198, 203.

6. As Budd points out in *Music and the Emotions*, p. 49.

7. Pratt, *The Meaning of Music*, p. 204.

8. Budd, *Music and the Emotions*, p. 50.

warranted by appeal to an account such as Pratt's is strictly limited.

I will call this kind of relation of musical movements to psychological states "co-nominal dynamic melisma": "melisma" because the kind of resemblance at issue is intention-neutral—that is, we may correctly describe as "jaunty" or "agitated" music whose composer had no such thought in mind; "dynamic" because the grounds for resemblance lie in movement; and "co-nominal" because the resemblance is not to a kind of behavior from which a psychological state can be inferred but to behavior that has the same name as, and is immediately constitutive of, such a state. Agitated music resembles not human movements that are expressive of agitation but rather human movements that are themselves, simply, agitated. The vocal melisma discussed at the beginning of the previous chapter, then, was all *non*–co-nominal—we hear anguish in Brahms's horn arpeggio because the music resembles a voice expressive of anguish, not because the music shares literally anguished qualities of sound with a voice. But examples of co-nominal vocal melisma can be found, too: music that resembles a "chirpy" human voice, for instance, shares with the voice a quality of sound that is immediately constitutive of, and has the same name as, the psychological state "chirpiness." Yet because (in our language) even fewer psychological states get their names from, and are defined in terms of, qualities of sound than those of motion, the range of co-nominal vocal melisma is likely to be very restricted indeed.

Co-nominal melisma, then—whether vocal or dynamic—is apt to be of quite limited interest to us, although its significance should not be underestimated even so. For I believe that the description of some music in psychological terms can be completely accounted for by reference to it. Domenico Scarlatti's Sonata in C, K. 502, for instance, is experienced as both jaunty and chirpy, and his Sonata in D minor, K. 517, as agitated and restless; yet neither work seems to invite further characterization in psychological language. But characterization as "jaunty," "restless" and so on is certainly too thin to make it likely that music as fascinating as Scarlatti's could possibly be fascinating on account of its capacity so to be characterized (or experienced). This suggests that co-nominal melisma is a minor phenomenon, not in the sense that it won't cover some (or even, I suspect, quite a lot of) music adequately, but in the sense that the music it does cover adequately is not very extensively, or most rewardingly, to be experienced under psychological concepts—which, to put it another way, is to say that some music (e.g., music whose psychological connotations can be captured entirely by appeal to the limited phenomenon of co-nominal melisma) does not significantly depend for its value upon its association with psychological states. And I think that reflection upon what it is like to enjoy, for example, Scarlatti's music will bear this out.

III

It is natural to wonder whether there is also a species of non–co-nominal dynamic melisma (hereafter simply "dynamic melisma") analogous to the melisma of Brahms's horn arpeggio, such that the movements of music resemble human movements expressive of certain passions, which passions are not named after those kinds of movements. Vocal melisma works because music can share with expressive human voices certain *distinctive* qualities of timbre, rhythm and contour; and we have seen in this chapter that music may also share with human beings many qualities of movement—some of which are qualities of expressive movement. An angry person moves abruptly and violently, a melancholy person slowly, and a proud one smoothly and expansively. Music, too, can move abruptly, violently, slowly, smoothly and expansively (the dead metaphor doesn't twitch). Can music, then, be melismatically expressive of anger, melancholy and pride? According to Eduard Hanslick it cannot; and it cannot simply because these qualities of movement are inadequately distinctive. In a famous passage he says:

> Music cannot represent the ideas of love, anger, fear, because between those ideas and beautiful combinations of tones there exists no necessary connection. Then which moment of these ideas is it that music knows how to seize so effectively? The answer is: motion. . . . Motion is the ingredient which music has in common with emotional states and which it is able to shape creatively in a thousand shades and contrasts. . . . What, then, makes a feeling specific, e.g., longing, love, hope? Is it perhaps the mere strength or weakness, the fluctuations of our inner activity? Certainly not. These can be similar with different feelings, and with the same feeling they can differ from person to person and from time to time. Only on the basis of a number of ideas and judgments (perhaps unconsciously at moments of strong feelings) can our state of mind congeal into this or that specific feeling. . . . Without them, without this cognitive apparatus, we cannot call the actual feeling "hope" or "melancholy"; . . . all that remains is an unspecific stirring, perhaps the awareness of a general state of well-being or distress. Love cannot be thought without the representation of a beloved person, without desire and striving after felicity, glorification and possession of a particular object. . . . Accordingly, its dynamic can appear as readily gentle as stormy, as readily joyful as sorrowful, and yet still be love. This consideration by itself suffices to show that music can only express the various accompanying adjectives, and never the substantive, e.g., love itself.[9]

So from the fact that the emotions may share dynamic qualities of "inner fluctuation" with one another ("animal spirits"

9. Edward Hanslick, *On the Musically Beautiful*, trans. G. Payzant (Indianapolis: Hackett, 1986), pp. 9–11.

again), and backed up by a cognitive account of emotion very similar to that offered here (in Chapter 1), Hanslick concludes that music cannot, by sharing certain of those dynamic qualities, be expressive of any *particular* emotion. Dynamic melisma, then (assuming Hanslick's strictures cover the motions of people's bodies as well as of their "animal spirits"), must be either impossible or else extremely vague.

This passage has been very influential, and the claim that dynamic qualities can be "similar with different feelings" does indeed constitute a powerful objection to the dynamic melisma account of musical expressiveness. But, of course, it does not follow from the fact that dynamic qualities may be "similar with different feelings" that no dynamic properties are peculiar to any feeling: for there may simply be an overlap of some qualities between feelings, while other qualities are distinctive of them. Yet even so, the objection looks persuasive. It is a good deal easier to spot cases of overlap (tumultuous movements for both terror and rage, for instance, or gentle movements for resignation and compassion) than it is to think of any movement that is unique to any feeling. But then again, it may be that it is not single dynamic qualities that are distinctive of particular feelings but combinations of dynamic qualities, in which case both the overlapping of qualities and the lack of individually distinctive qualities would be compatible with music's being expressive of specific passions. It is this suggestion which we must now try to evaluate. In doing so, however, we will progress best if we observe certain constraints, particularly on the kinds of example that we use. For the hypothesis we have in mind suggests that it is in virtue of music's dynamic properties *alone* that music might be expressive of specific passions, which means that we will be well advised to confine our attentions to music whose expressive properties appear to be predominantly dynamic. If we concentrate on songs, for example, or on music accompanied by long explanatory texts, or by actions on stage, we risk mistaking the expressive effects of words or actions for the effects of musical dynamics. We do better, then, for our present purposes, and if we wish to assess the position adopted by Hanslick, to concentrate on pure instrumental music, with as little extramusical expressive import as may be convenient. The suggestion we want to evaluate—that combinations of dynamic qualities may be distinctive of particular feelings, and that these dynamic qualities may be found in music—lies at the heart of an attempt by Donald Ferguson to explicate the workings of expressive music.

Ferguson begins by distinguishing three elements in emotional experience: a "feeling-tone," which involves a measure of tension; an impulse toward certain characteristic kinds of motion; and a context, which is the object of the emotion (or the object of the ideas and judgments in Hanslick's "cognitive apparatus"). The experience is most clearly defined when all three elements are present; but the first two are sufficient to mark the emotion off as distinctive.[10] Now music cannot, of course, portray or present the context of an emotional experience. But it can capture the elements of tension and motion very well, and may thus, according to Ferguson, portray or present enough of the experience to distinguish the emotion it involves from other emotions: "Dynamic emphasis . . . may suggest distinctive characteristics of physical or nervous energy; and all these features, conjoined with the intrinsic motor-impulses of consonant or dissonant harmony, may embody the depicted motion in an apparently corporeal musical mass whose weight and volume may be adjusted (as, for instance, no dancer's body could be adjusted) to the portrayal . . . of the vital impulse to motion activating a sentient being."[11] But he does not dispense

10. Donald Ferguson, *Music as Metaphor* (Minneapolis: University of Minnesota Press, 1960), p. 53.
11. Ibid., p. 75.

with the third contextual element altogether; for he believes that if the dynamic part of an experience is "vividly portrayed, it is conceivable that a plausible inference may be drawn therefrom as to the nature of the experience itself."[12] So he believes that the object of an emotional experience can be deduced from other aspects of that experience, so that its full character may become evident. The process of musical expression, he says, is the "converse of that employed by the so-called representative arts. These begin with portrayed circumstance which, as we apprehend it, generates by a kind of inference its feeling-correlative. Our proposed process begins with the portrayed feeling which generates an inference of appropriate . . . circumstance."[13] But this is a little misleading; for certainly Ferguson ought not to be claiming that the inference will yield a circumstance of comparable particularity to those that might be portrayed by the representational arts. If music portrays a feeling of exultation, say, it would be absurd to attribute that feeling to something specific, like an unwarrantedly high mark for a chemistry test, or the fall of a despot (which might be represented in the other arts). Rather—and in line with remarks made here at the end of Chapter 1—"appropriate circumstance" must mean appropriate *type* of circumstance, so that from the feeling of exultation only "*something* fantastically welcome" is inferred, not what: music may be expressive of emotion types, formally construed, not of particular episodes of emotion, materially construed (e.g., episodes having exam results or tyrants for object).

So can this expressive process be shown to work? Ferguson offers several examples in its support, but the most detailed and convincing is taken from the opening of the *Eroica*'s funeral march.[14]

12. Ibid., p. 53.
13. Ibid., p. 55.
14. Ibid., pp. 106ff.

Beethoven, Symphony no. 3 in E♭, Op. 55 (*Eroica*): second
movement, opening bars

Ferguson must establish the expressive character of these bars
by attempting first to separate from them their elements of
tension and motion and then by relating these to the same
elements of some specific emotion. He examines first the element of motion. The rhythmic propulsion of the passage is
striking, with each of the first five bars beginning with notes
of "identical and impressive length—notes which absorb into
themselves the considerable propulsive force supplied by the
appoggiatura figure in the basses and by the initial up-beat, so
that the weight of these notes is extraordinary." This force is
however virtually exhausted in the appoggiaturas preceding the
first G quarter note in the treble, leaving the second half of the
first bar to generate on its own the momentum required to
reach the next strong beat. In the slow tempo, the dotted
sixteenths followed by thirty-seconds lend a "sense of labor-
iousness to the ascent; and this sense is augmented by the fall of
the long E♭ to C." The effort needed to attain the E♭ (a climb of,
overall, only a minor third) is emphasized by its failure, upon

receiving renewed propulsive force from the appoggiaturas, to do anything but subside again. The moment of silence that follows—at the end of bar 2—suggests a pause, after these labors, for rest. The rhythmic thrust that again starts the third bar does so this time out of the silence of bar 2, and this gives to the following high G, "in comparison to all the preceding tones, an almost explosive energy. But again this energy is absorbed into the note," and the descent ensues once more, this time sounding almost precipitous, for the distance, a fifth, is more than twice that of the earlier fall. The impression is strengthened further by the reversal of the rhythm of ascent in the first bar. Now the dotted sixteenth notes come after the thirty-seconds: "The whole sense of forward progression in the musical substance . . . is extremely retarded. Its motion is dragged and weighted, heavy-footed and slow; yet the sense of underlying energy is abundant, so that there is no rhythmic sense of weakness or defeat."

The element of tension is in accord with the element of motion, and contributes to the impressions already outlined. The accented notes in the first two bars are all "rest tones"—that is, they are the tones of the tonic triad, in this case C minor: C, E♭ and G. Any other tones are "active tones," which demand resolution—i.e. movement to one of the rest tones. The ubiquity of rest tones on the important beats of the first two bars, then, imparts a stability that "contributes greatly to the sense of weight which we found to be illustrated by the music in its motor aspect." This sense of weight is heightened in the next two bars. The high G, attacked out of nothing, is so heavy as to function almost as an active tone (but imagine a truly "active tone—for example, an A♭—and consider the immediate loss in dignity and character!"); and the downward motion is emphasized, not only by the rhythmic reversal noted above but by "the placing of the rhythmic accent on the active tones . . . which gain only a precarious foothold on the unaccented rest tones to which they fall." The D in the fourth bar is the first really conspicuous active note, but from there until the full cadence in bar 8 almost all the accented notes are now active. The high A♭ in bar 6 parallels the G in bar 4, but instead of exploding out of silence its intensity is prepared by an ascending set of active dotted sixteenth notes alternating with thirty-seconds on rest tones. (And, as Ferguson might have added, the preceding figure in the basses, no longer appoggiatural, now descends for the only time in the passage—to the lowest accented note yet— to give to the A♭ above an additional intensity: the distance between bass and treble is here, suddenly, at its greatest.) The A♭ "conveys an indubitable sense of pain, [but] its momentary outcry is dominated at once by the extraordinary firmness of the conclusion of the whole theme," an effect accomplished by the rhythmically even sixteenths in the seventh bar.

The harmony augments the impression further. For the first three and a half bars a C-minor chord is presented in successive inversions, culminating in a $^6_4$ preparing the half-cadence. Although unrelieved, "it imparts great firmness and dignity. Instead of appearing monotonous, it supports and enhances the directness of the melodic utterance, precluding any suggestion of . . . nervous abandon." The next two bars are supported by a single active harmony—the diminished seventh—before the C-minor triad returns, so that the cadence, "harmonically as well as rhythmically, is on a note of resolute firmness": "This is more than mere marching-music for the dead. Its solemnity is as profound as its sadness. Grief permeates every note and every rhythmic step; but there is no yielding—no indulgence in the alleviating misery of tears. It comprehends heroically and is unafraid."[15] Thus Ferguson completes his survey of these eight bars, with an eloquent summation of their total expressive effect. His description of the patterns of tension and motion is persuasive, showing how all the elements pull together in the same direction—at the beginning and at the end toward sta-

15. Ibid., p. 109.

bility, and in bars 5 and 6 toward a greater sense of tension; and perhaps the only false note intrudes when he says that the harmony of the first half precludes any suggestion of "nervous abandon"; it is hard to imagine the possibility having arisen.

The trouble, of course, is that it is not clear whether the description of patterns of tension and motion actually warrants the summation of expressive effect that is offered. For it is an easy matter to tell a very different story about the dynamics of Beethoven's eight bars. Imagine a miniature terrain of successive escarpments. The first is lower than the second and is separated from it by a rampart, or a lip, and a short stretch of level ground. At the bottom is a beetle. It pushes before itself a little ball of dung, in a stolid and unimaginative fashion. It begins to labor up the first slope (bar 1), but after the beetle gets just about a third of the way up, the ball—which is awkwardly heavy—rolls back to the bottom again (bar 2). With a determined thrust the beetle shoves it back up (bar 3), and this time it gets almost to the top before falling (bar 4). The beetle interrupts its descent just above the bottom of the slope, and with a new and more lively action it jerks the ball upward (bar 5). On this occasion it gets it to the top, and, after a moment's teetering on the rampart (the A♭ in bar 6), the ball bounces firmly over onto the level ground before the second escarpment (bars 7 and 8). This story fits the dynamic patterns of the music exactly: so what reason might we have to prefer a summation like Ferguson's to one that extols the perseverance of beetles?

The first thing to say is that because music lacks the representational capacity of the other arts it is unlikely to be able to represent well something so specific as a beetle and a ball of dung. From the dynamic patterns we might just as well have inferred a beaver and a log, or a ginger-haired pirate called Ian and the priceless hoard of Marakesh. But *whichever* we had chosen, the outlines of the story—as dictated by the motions of the music—would have been much the same. And the qualities displayed, whether by beetle, beaver or Ian, would also have been similar: perseverance, fortitude, firmness—things like that. Instead of telling a story, then, which must necessarily involve a degree of invention that music's representational capacities can never underwrite, and which is therefore redundant, we do better to isolate what is common to any story that will fit the pattern. This is effectively what Ferguson has done. But what is the justification for relating these patterns to *passions* or *states of mind* (which is what the beetle story implicitly does too), rather than to instances of movement in general? This is a problem that did not arise over vocal melisma; and it did not arise there simply because the sounds that music was held uncomplicatedly to resemble were the sounds of the human voice—and no one doubts that the human voice is expressive of passion. Dynamic melisma, on the other hand, presents music as resembling (also relatively uncomplicatedly) certain of the qualities of movement possessed by moving things, among which—but obviously not all of which—are human bodies moving expressively; yet other moving bodies may have no expressive qualities at all.

Hanslick says that between the dynamics of passion "and beautiful combinations of tones there exists no necessary connection."[16] And that is what we have just seen. But he also says, of the "harmonious dying away" of an adagio, that the "imagination, which gladly refers artistic ideas to the peculiarly human inner awareness, will interpret this dying away on a higher level, e.g., as the expression of mellow resignation by a person of equable disposition"[17]—which, although he somewhat regrets it, he is unquestionably right about. It is because the imagination does this that the psychological language of Ferguson's summation does not strike us as being out of place. I am not sure, however, that it is possible adequately to justify or explain this imaginative habit of ours. It is maybe just a brute fact about us. But because music, as a product of human activity, belongs

16. Hanslick, *On The Musically Beautiful*, p. 11.
17. Ibid., p. 10.

to that class of objects most naturally to be interpreted in psychological terms, and because music can move us and can powerfully affect our own states of mind, and because vocal melisma and co-nominal melisma already provide a direct connection between music and psychological description, it is perhaps not a very surprising fact about us. Indeed, even when we interpret musical movement more pictorially—as portraying a storm, for instance, or the babbling of a brook—our interpretation is not without psychological connotations. Storms, in or out of music, are "furious"; and babbling brooks are "bright and cheerful." This is why Beethoven could describe his (rather pictorial) "Pastoral" Symphony as "more feeling than painting."

So let us accept the privileged role of psychological description in Ferguson's analysis of the funeral march. I think it will be clear even so that his summation claims more than his analysis warrants. The descriptions of motion that apply most persuasively to the march are those such as "slow," "heavy," "steady," "measured," "effortful," "unyielding," "propelled from beneath," "limited in range" and so on. These descriptions are certainly compatible with the motions of a sad or solemn person, and might warrant Ferguson's claim that the music's "solemnity is as profound as its sadness." (Indeed, the sad quality of the passage is emphasized when, in the next eight bars, the plaintive sound of the oboe—vocal melisma—takes up the theme an octave higher.) But his claim that "grief permeates every note" cannot be justified in the same way; for the difference between grief and profound sadness is that grief quite specifically involves the loss of something loved, and the movements of music could never suggest *that*. "It comprehends heroically and is unafraid," he says. But it is not clear which of the music's movements are supposed to resemble the movements of a "heroic comprehension"; in fact, it is not clear that a "heroic comprehension" could possibly have characteristic movements to resemble. The only questionable point in the analysis itself is when we are told that the high A♭ "conveys an indubitable sense of pain"; for at first this looks equally difficult to attribute to any motion pattern. Certainly the A♭ conveys an indubitable sense of tension, as a result of the widely spaced diminished seventh harmony beneath it. Yet it can perhaps be argued that in a slow passage of sad and solemn music such as this, tensions are bound to come across as painful (add tension to sadness and you get something worse); and in the sense that sadness simply *is* painful, it would be surprising if a prominent moment in a sad passage were not painful.

But this consideration does little to help out Ferguson's summation of the expressive effect of the whole. The fact is that the context—that is, the element of passionate experience which defines it most closely—has not been inferred from the dynamic patterns. It has been provided by the title of the movement—*marcia funebre*—which means that the full expressive character claimed for the music derives significantly from nondynamic aspects of the music. Of *course* any sadness in a funereal context is most likely to be grief; and one whose movements at a funeral are grieving, and yet "steady," "measured" and "unyielding" too, exhibits an acceptance of death which, if not necessarily "heroically comprehending," is certainly dignified. So the summation offered depends upon Beethoven's music being a funeral march—as in general there is no reason why it shouldn't, since it is one. But this dependence does make somewhat equivocal the support that such an example can give to a theory like Ferguson's, which is supposed to rest upon dynamics alone—which is supposed to show, contra Hanslick, that music all by itself, in the absence of words, texts or actions, is capable of being expressive of specific passions.

We can salvage, however, from his account the descriptions of motion that his analysis has shown to fit the music. These, in combination, describe the dynamic character of the whole eight bars. They do not describe successive episodes: the quoted passage forms a single dynamic span that is, in toto, slow, steady, measured, heavy, effortful, unyielding, propelled from beneath,

limited in range, dignified and firm. Now it is clear that although many of these descriptions might individually fit many
different passions, taken together they are unlikely to be very
versatile, to be "similar with different feelings." For the kind of
movement they collectively describe is a very specific kind of
movement; and no one would think that a way of moving that
was slow, steady, measured and so on betokened glee, for example, or anxiety or indecision or gaiety. Such a way of moving
could only make one think of a state of mind that was both
on the unhappy side, and also resolute. This shows that inasmuch as our imagination does "gladly" refer "artistic ideas to
the peculiarly human inner awareness" it does not do so uncon-
strainedly—but in accordance with a perception of a highly
particular form of movement that only a limited range of
feelings could conceivably share. Therefore, provided that we
do not require a summation as elaborate as Ferguson's, the
combination of dynamic qualities which he has demonstrated
may provide a basis for a species of dynamic melisma that is far
less vague than Hanslick's strictures would have led one to
expect.

IV

The most natural name, I think—and one which provokes no
metaphorical twitchings—for a passage of music of a single,
specific, dynamic span (like Beethoven's eight bars), and whose
quality of motion is to be captured by a unified combination of
dynamic descriptions, is a *gesture*—a *musical gesture*. A musical
gesture, then, is somewhat like a musical phrase in its dynamic
aspect. Ferguson clearly has a similar thought in mind when he
says that music "may embody the depicted motion in an apparently corporeal mass whose weight and volume may be adjusted
(as, for instance no dancer's body could be adjusted) to the
portrayal . . . of the vital impulse to motion activating a sentient
being"; for dance is nothing if not gesture. But musical gestures
may also have an aspect that the physical gestures of a dancer

must lack—a vocal aspect. For musical gestures may be both—
that is, at the same time, dynamically *and* vocally melismatic
(which, in effect, renders music operatic in advance of any
opera). So their potential for precision, or for great particularity, is even richer than Ferguson allows.

But it is important not to misconstrue the *kind* of precision
that musical gestures may have. For example, in their melismatic effects they do not necessarily stand in precise one-to-one
correspondences with states of mind that we can readily name
(such as sadness, for instance, or terror). The first eight bars
of the *marcia funebre* constitute an extremely precise musical
gesture—indeed an infinitely precise gesture: *any* change in the
music would alter its character. And yet we cannot at all easily
say just *which* state of mind it corresponds to. Hanslick was
right about that part. But we can certainly indicate quite well
the general type of psychological state—as unhappy, say, but
resolute—that the musical gesture brings to mind. The musical
gesture is therefore precise in just the way that a physical gesture
is precise. A person's gestures may communicate what is felt in a
way that his or her words cannot, and in a way for which we
may find it impossible to formulate a verbal paraphrase. Yet if
those gestures assume only a very slightly different (dynamic)
character, then the state of mind which is revealed may change
markedly—but again, in a way that we find it very difficult to
describe. The precision of the gesture, therefore, lies in its
uniqueness. Two distinct gestures may bring to mind psychological states that we would describe in the same words, and yet
we know that they do not stand for the same state: for one
gesture, *this* gesture, reveals one state, and *that* gesture reveals
another. And it is a failure of language (or of our own grasp of
language) if we cannot capture that difference in words. When
asked to say what a piece of his music was expressive of, Schumann is reported to have sat back down at the piano and played
it again, as if to say, "That." And if musical gestures are like
physical gestures, then this was a very proper response. It is the

particularity of the gesture that explains why all musical expressiveness has been said, I think incoherently, to be "intransitive"[18]—and that explains, too, why Mendelssohn said that "a piece of music that I love expresses thoughts to me that are not too *imprecise* to be framed in words, but too *precise*. So I find that attempts to express such thoughts in words may have some point to them, but they are also unsatisfying."[19]

But perhaps this is to rush ahead, rather. For there is a difference between musical and physical gestures that has not been mentioned. The difference is simply that we *know* that a person is the kind of thing that can have a state of mind which gestures may reveal. People can have episodes of emotion, directed toward clearly identifiable material objects ("material" in Kenny's sense), which their gestures can make manifest; indeed their gestures themselves may identify the object of the emotion by, for example, hitting it or stroking it (but only if the object is material in both senses). But music is not the kind of thing that can have a state of mind to reveal; and certainly insofar as music can resemble melismatically a person's expressive gestures, or the qualities of a voice, these musical gestures—be they never so precise—can show neither the existence nor the identity of any material object, which is to say that they can never reveal an episode of emotion. As I have suggested, then, music's melismatic repertoire must be confined to a semblance of expression in a *formal* sense—a sense analogous to that in which the behavior of a person who *practices* looking exultant presents a semblance of behavior expressive of exultance. Such a person merely behaves *as if* in response to something fantastically welcome; but because there is no particular thing that is fantastically welcome, the behavior can truly express neither *this* exultance nor

18. By, e.g., Alan Tormey, *The Concept of Expression* (Princeton: Princeton University Press, 1971), part 2.

19. Quoted in Peter le Huray and James Day, eds., *Music and Aesthetics in the Eighteenth and Early Nineteenth Centuries* (Cambridge: Cambridge University Press, 1988), p. 311.

that. And so it is with music. This means that while a physical (nonpractice) gesture can very precisely convey a very precise state of mind (so that the precision of the gesture and the precision of the state of mind are mutually dependent), a musical gesture (or a practice physical gesture), because it may only present a formal semblance of expressive behavior, can only (very precisely) convey a *kind* of state of mind (so that the precision of the gesture *outstrips* the precision of the state of mind, because the gesture is not a function of it). Thus, music may adjust its gestures as "no dancer's body could be adjusted," without the precision and the particularity achieved thereby revealing any precise or particular state of mind—in the *marcia funebre,* for instance, nothing more precise than "on the unhappy side, and also resolute."

I have suggested, then, that certain of the expressive features of music are those that share qualities of sound with the human expressive voice and qualities of movement with human expressive behavior. And I should probably enter a reminder here that such musical features may include *harmonic* features: for harmony is integral to many melismatic gestures. We saw in Chapter 3 that the perceptual properties of a musical experience may combine with and modify one another. The harmonic properties of an experience may therefore combine with and modify its melodic properties—properties that, of course, are the most obviously relevant to musical melisma. Thus the varieties of human expressive behavior that a melismatic gesture resembles may depend upon the way in which the melodic aspect of that gesture has been harmonized (as Ferguson shows in his analysis of the *marcia funebre*). The perceptual property of harmony may also combine with and modify the perceptual property of timbre—and this is of significance for vocal melisma. Thus harmony, as well as melody, rhythm and timbre, may contribute to the resemblance between music and human expressive behavior. (Of course, harmony may also be expressive by reason of *convention.* Indeed, it is probable that harmony is conventionally expressive more often than it is melismatically expressive: I can't think of a persuasive melismatic explanation for the sadness of minor chords, for example, or for the expressive effect of certain harmonic progressions.) I don't want to claim that the features I have mentioned are music's only expressive features; but I do think that they are some of its most important ones. The type of expressiveness that I attribute to music on account of these features is melismatic expressiveness; and I have argued that such expressiveness can be expressive of only general *kinds* of states of mind. Thus, if a piece of music is melismatically expressive of sadness, then it may be expressive of sadness in an infinitely particular way but still not, on the account offered so far, expressive of any particular sadness. The expressive gesture is an individual; the state conveyed is not.

I have already quoted Schopenhauer's remark that "music does not express this or that particular and definite pleasure, this or that affliction, . . . but joy, pain, sorrow, [etc.] *themselves*, to a certain extent in the abstract, their essential nature, without any accessories, and so also without the motives for them." But I might equally well have quoted Susanne Langer's assertion that "what music can actually reflect is only the morphology of feeling; and it is quite plausible that [different] . . . conditions may have a very similar morphology"; or Kendall Walton, when he says that "music has a tendency to express properties— universals rather than particulars."[20] This common intuition is, I believe, explained rather fully by the remarks I have offered here about the melismatic musical gesture. But melisma isn't really a matter of expression. It is a species of resemblance. And I believe that it is only when we have moved beyond mere melisma that we shall be able to make sense of the other kind of intuition—Mendelssohn's kind, or Malcolm Budd's when he

20. Susanne Langer, *Philosophy in a New Key* (Cambridge: Harvard University Press, 1971), p. 238; and Kendall Walton, "What Is Abstract about the Art of Music?" *Journal of Aesthetics and Art Criticism* (1988): 362n.

says that "much expressive music is heard as containing states of mind that create the impression of a personality."[21] *That* will require music to be expressive not merely of, for example, no particular sadness in an infinitely particular way, but of *this* and *that* infinitely particular sadness. An attempt to move beyond melismatic resemblance, and hence to capture more fully the thought behind this other intuition, will therefore constitute the greater part of the final three chapters.

21. Budd, *Music and the Emotions*, p. 149.

CHAPTER SIX

Musical Sympathies

For what can be more strange, than that the rubbing of a little
Hair and Cat-gut together, shou'd make such a mighty
alteration in a Man that sits at a distance?
— JEREMY COLLIER, *Essays upon Several Subjects*

Given that music is capable of being expressive, and given that
there appear to be good reasons for supposing that melisma is
to some degree responsible for that capability, we must now
address two difficulties that a melisma-based account of expressiveness in music must overcome. First, there is the problem
that melisma is not by itself capable of underwriting the degree
of expressive *precision* so prized by Mendelssohn and others.
Music is poor at representing persons, things, ideas or states of
affairs; and so the melismatic gesture is unable to resemble
behavior expressive of responses *to* persons, things, ideas or
states of affairs. All that music can do is resemble, in an infinitely particular way, pieces of expressive behavior in isolation
from the contexts in which what they express is fully distinctive—in which what they express is *this* passion rather than *that*.
The second problem is that melisma itself isn't expressive—it
only *resembles* something expressive. Thus, while melisma may
well be *responsible* for our experience of music as expressive, it
cannot by itself explain what it *is* to experience music as expressive.[1] To offer an account of musical expressiveness wholly in

1. A point emphasized by both Malcolm Budd and Jerrold Levinson, in their
reviews of Peter Kivy's *The Corded Shell* (Princeton: Princeton University Press,

terms of melisma, then, would be like offering an account of
pictorial space wholly in terms of the perspectival devices contained by a picture: it might be true that we experience pictorial
space *in virtue* of the perspectival devices that a picture contains; but the experience itself is not merely the experience of
perceiving perspectival devices (which one could have without
ever experiencing pictorial space). It is an experience of volume
and depth—qualities not of the devices themselves, or of the
perception of them, but of the space that they enable one to
experience. In the same way, the experience of music as expressive is not merely the experience of hearing melismatic gestures
(which one could have without ever experiencing music as
expressive). It is an experience having perceptual qualities that
are qualities not of melisma, or of the perception of it, but of the
expressiveness that melisma enables one to experience. The
attempt to characterize *that* experience, then, must inevitably
take us beyond melisma itself.

I

In Chapter 4 I made a distinction between theories that construe music as simply melismatic and those that attribute to
music, in virtue of the melismatic resemblance of certain of its
features to motions of the impassioned "animal spirits," the
capacity to arouse in a listener the passions corresponding to
those motions. This second kind of theory is usually known as
an "arousal theory" of musical expressiveness. Because the simply melismatic option has proved insufficient, it will be as well
to investigate the alternative. For if the experience of listening to
some music involves passionate response as well as "purely
musical" and melismatic properties it is possible that the more
complex experience so characterized will be of such a kind as to
account for the association of that music with passions of great

1980). Budd's review is in the *Times Literary Supplement* (1981): 762; Levinson's
review is in *Canadian Philosophical Reviews* (1981): 150.

precision. It is not, of course, necessary in order to investigate this suggestion to subscribe to a philosophy of mind that takes seriously the idea of the "animal spirits." It is necessary only to take seriously the thought that music may move us, and that it may do so in virtue of its melismatic properties. My intention is, in effect, to test one sense of Nelson Goodman's claim that "in aesthetic experience the emotions function cognitively."[2] For if our passionate responses to a piece of music sometimes contribute to the precision of our characterization of that music in psychological terms, the cognitive function of such responses must play a part in any convincing account of the relation between music and the passions.

The claim that our musical experience does sometimes involve the arousal of passionate response is not a very controversial one. Such a claim is certainly in accord with the common-sense view; and it also enjoys quite a wide acceptance among philosophers of music.[3] It is less clear, though, what exactly follows from, or is involved in, the fact of impassioned arousal. There are at least two ways of interpreting our affective responses to music which will disqualify them at once from functioning in the cognitive fashion that interests us. The first construes those responses as generically special, so that they cannot be of such a kind as to qualify or augment the description of music in psychological terms based on its melismatic properties; for such description makes no appeal to generically special psychological states. Such theories, which claim that we are aroused to sui generis, or peculiarly musical, affective states, seem to me to be implausible from every angle, and I won't

2. Nelson Goodman, *Languages of Art* (Indianapolis: Hackett, 1968), p. 248.

3. See, e.g., Stephen Davies, "The Rationality of Aesthetic Responses," *British Journal of Aesthetics* (1983): 38–47; Jerrold Levinson, "Music and Negative Emotion," *Pacific Philosophical Quarterly* (1982): 327–46; and Colin Radford, "Emotions and Music: A Reply to the Cognitivists," *Journal of Aesthetics and Art Criticism* (1989): 69–76.

discuss them here: they have been well dealt with elsewhere.[4] But I do want to say something about the other (unhelpful) class of ways of interpreting our affective responses to music, ways that are guilty of the heresy of the separable experience— the heresy of representing "a musical work as being related in a certain way to an experience which can be fully characterized [and valued] without reference to the nature of the work itself."[5] Any version guilty of the heresy will be unable to participate in an account of musical expressiveness that aims, in part, to explain why we value some music *for* its expressiveness; and I hope that my account will, in part, be able to do that.

A first heretical version of the "arousal theory" construes passionate responses to music as *associative* responses (which, as we saw in Chapter 2, are more or less bound to be heretical). Peter Kivy, for example, attributes arousal to "the images and remembrances of things past which the music stimulates." This is

confirmed by my own experience of what is essentially the "our song" phenomenon. Mahler's *Knaben Wunderhorn* never fails to make me feel a bit off color when I hear it nowadays, even the "happy" parts, because it is associated with a particularly unhappy period of my life which it invariably calls to mind. No one should doubt that music can and does arouse emotions in this way. What we deny is that this has anything to do with musical expressiveness. And the fact that so much of the power that music does have to arouse the emotions is due to private idiosyncratic associations is itself additional reason for rejecting the arousal theory altogether as a theory of musical expressiveness.[6]

If it were true that *all* arousal is "due to private, idiosyncratic associations"—which is what Kivy seems to mean (and is what

4. See Levinson, "Music and Negative Emotion," pp. 329–34.
5. Malcolm Budd, *Music and the Emotions* (London: R. K. P., 1985), p. 123.
6. Kivy, *The Corded Shell*, p. 30.

Renée Cox, for example, says explicitly[7])—then I think that it would be right to say that the arousal theory must be rejected altogether as a theory of musical expressiveness. The theory would be rank with heresy. But it is not true that all arousal is associative. The difference between my response to the *Abscheid* from Mahler's *Das Lied von der Erde* and my response to the finale of Mozart's "Jupiter" Symphony certainly does not derive from differences between the images or memories that they respectively conjure up. My different responses seem instead to be explicable in terms of the different melismatic qualities I detect in those works. Of course, it is open to Kivy to argue that it is precisely these melismatic differences that make me associate the Mahler with one set of memories and the Mozart with another. But if I deny, as I do, that I associate either work with *any* memories in the relevant way, then it is difficult to know what he might say. An appeal to unconscious association would clearly be pointless; if my responses can be elucidated by reference to the music's melismatic properties then there is no need for additional explanation at the unconscious level—nor is there any further role of an explanatory kind that association might play. Moreover, the fact that the same work in different performances can arouse subtly different feelings is, on the association model, inexplicable. The difference in response is due to the difference in performance; but I cannot possibly associate different performances with different images and memories, for unless the performances are recorded I have never previously heard them. None of this, of course, is to say that associative response is not for some listeners the only form of affective response a musical experience can afford. It is merely to say that for other listeners other kinds of response are possible.

7. Renée Cox, "Varieties of Musical Expressionism," in George Dickie, Richard Sclafani and Ronald Roblin, eds., *Aesthetics: A Critical Anthology*, 2d ed. (New York: St. Martin's Press, 1988), pp. 604–14.

A rather different account is suggested by Hindemith, who claims that the feelings that music arouses cannot be real feelings, for "real feelings need a certain interval of time to develop, to reach a climax, and to fade out again; but reactions to music may change as fast as musical phrases do, they may spring up in full intensity at any given moment and disappear entirely when the musical pattern which provokes them ends or changes."[8] "We know the reason for this," he says: "The emotions released by music are no real emotions, they are mere images of emotion that have been experienced before, . . . [and not] the real, untransformed, and unmodified feelings."[9] Thus, music "releases" a series of remembered "emotion-images." This is not straightforwardly an account of associative response, of course; but it has in common with such an account the claim that what music arouses are passions, or "emotion-images," which derive from the past experience of the listener; and if Hindemith means by this that music simply stimulates "images and remembrances of things past," and that these depend only upon the temperament and personal history of the listener, then such images will be idiosyncratic and only contingently related to the music that occasions them. The remarks made above about Kivy's suggestion will then apply equally here. But if, on the other hand, Hindemith means that emotion-images can be "released" *only* by music, and that they are "released" *only* as a result of paying close attention to the "musical pattern," then the experience of emotion-images that he describes will be ineliminably an experience of the music itself—will refer, that is, to no contingent or separable experience. If, further, he means that when the listener's past experience happens not to contain an emotion of a certain kind, the listener experiences no emotion-image at the corresponding point in the music, then

8. Paul Hindemith, *A Composer's World* (Cambridge: Harvard University Press, 1952), p. 45.

9. Ibid., p. 49.

there is no reason to think that the emotion-images the listener *does* experience are private or idiosyncratic, on Hindemith's account: for the listener will experience either appropriate emotion-images or none at all. But even if this *is* what Hindemith means, or can be construed to mean, there are problems. In the first place, his emotion-images must be more than mere memories if they are to be a form of passionate response at all; but if they *are* a form of passionate response, then there seems to be no particular reason to distinguish them (as "images") from passions proper. And second, as Deryck Cooke has pointed out, music may make a listener *"feel as he has never felt before"*[10]— and in ways that he might struggle to describe; it simply isn't true that our passionate responses are *always* reruns of our earlier passionate experiences. So Hindemith's account, even when interpreted so that the heresy of the separable experience is avoided, cannot be made to yield an adequate account of passionate response to music—which shows that a plausible version of the arousal theory must clearly be a version that exploits passionate responses other than those due to private association, however construed.

A second heretical form of the arousal theory (which I shall call the "strong" form) holds that the capacity of music to arouse feeling exhausts the meaning of all description of music in affective terms.[11] To call music expressive, on this theory, is simply to attribute to it a disposition to arouse feeling in its listeners. The focus is on *causes* of arousal, rather than reasons—which doubtless explains the attachment felt by psychologists of music to a strong arousal theory.[12] But clearly such a theory is

10. Deryck Cooke, *The Language of Music* (Oxford: Oxford University Press, 1959), p. 19.

11. See, e.g., Peter Mew, "The Expression of Emotion in Music," *British Journal of Aesthetics* (1985): 33–42—to which I have responded in "Mr. Mew on Music," *British Journal of Aesthetics* (1986): 69–70.

12. See, e.g., John Davies, *The Psychology of Music* (Stanford: Stanford University Press, 1978), pp. 62–72.

not a theory of expressiveness at all. To ascribe dispositional predicates to a thing is not to attribute to it any expressive qualities. We need not, for example, think expressive of irritation a dentist who, irritatingly, hurts us—though it might be true that the dentist is irritating. Therefore a proponent of the strong arousal theory is committed to the claim that music is not expressive at all; the fact that we say it is just a linguistic muddle. By itself, of course, this does not show that there is anything wrong with the strong arousal theory. Linguistic muddles happen. But it does make certain things difficult to account for. A dentist is only irritating if he produces irritation: yet we can and do describe pieces of music as jolly even if we feel nothing when we listen to them. On the strong arousal theory such descriptions would be straightforwardly false. Further, we can find a jolly piece of music acutely irritating just *because* of its jollity. But if it were true, as the strong arousal theory maintains, that states aroused exhaust the meaning of descriptions of music in affective terms, then that piece of music would simply *be* irritating, and no reference to jollity could arise (or be warranted). Thus the *reason* for our irritation eludes the theory. The strong arousal theory, then, doesn't merely offer to rectify a linguistic muddle; it interprets plausible claims as self-evidently false, and it renders implausible our (perfectly good) reasons for making them. Thus the theory misrepresents our experience of music and even (as in the case of irritatingly jolly music) misrepresents our experience of the musical arousal of affect. An acceptable arousal theory, then, can't be of the strong kind.

I said, when discussing the association model of arousal, that I thought I could explain the differences between my responses to different pieces of music by reference to the differences in melisma that those pieces contained. And I argued just now that the description of music in affective terms could not be reduced without remainder to the ascription to music of dispositions to arouse feeling. These two thoughts fit together directly. Consider again the case of irritatingly jolly music. What I think is really going on here is that jollity is being ascribed to the music on melismatic grounds: the music is, elliptically, being called jolly because its gestures resemble behavior expressive of jollity; and the "irritating" ascription is coming from an aroused response to the (formally characterized) jollity that the music melismatically brings to mind (or perhaps to other, nonmelismatic, qualities of the music's melismatic gestures). Thus, there is an experience of both melisma *and* arousal; and I believe that it is this complex experience which a successful arousal theory must elucidate. I shall attempt to develop such a theory (a "weak" arousal theory) in the next two sections.

II

If, when I listen to the *marcia funebre*, it makes me feel heavyhearted but resolute, then my affective response has much the same character as the general state of which the behavior that the music resembles is expressive. It has that character in virtue of my experience of the music's gestures as melismatic. In an elliptical sense I can describe the music as expressive of heavyhearted resolution on the strength of melisma alone (the description is elliptical, for "the music resembles behavior expressive of some state of heavyhearted resolution"). Such descriptions are like those established by Ferguson in the analysis we looked at in the preceding chapter. But what happens in the experience of the *marcia funebre* as (nonelliptically) expressive, I believe, is that in attending to the musical gestures I come to be aware of their heavyhearted, resolute quality through the very process of coming myself to feel heavyhearted but resolute.[13] It is rather like my coming to appreciate the melancholy of a weeping willow only as the willow saddens me: I could, of course, merely identify the expressive posture that the willow's posture resembles; but instead I apprehend its melancholy

13. This suggestion has an obvious affinity with Stephen Davies's idea of "mirroring responses": see "The Expression of Emotion in Music," *Mind* (1980): 67–86.

through a kind of mirroring response. I respond to it *sympathetically*. Nor need there be anything troublingly private or idiosyncratic about my response. For my response is grounded in the resemblance that the willow bears to a particular human expressive posture; and that resemblance can be shown, teased out, made explicit. Thus sympathetic response, unlike associative response, is open to certain forms of *public* assessment. Associative responses can only be idiosyncratic, never appropriate or inappropriate. Whereas a sympathetic response can be shown to be more or less well suited to the object that has occasioned it.

I said that I *believed* that the experience of music as expressive involves a sympathetic or mirroring response. And I should probably come clean here and admit that the most compelling reason I have for believing this derives not from any argument, or from any set of conceptual considerations, but simply from reflection upon what my own experience of expressive music seems to be like. This clearly leaves me vulnerable to objections from those who interpret their musical experiences differently. But the claim that music can be moving—that listening to melancholy music can make one melancholy, or that hearing happy music can cheer one up—surely reflects no very aberrant kind of musical experience. Indeed, such a claim would seem to square readily with the common-sense, pretheoretical beliefs about music that most listeners actually have. If we can make sense of that claim, then, we will have good cause to accept it (on the excellent grounds that we reject a common-sense belief at our peril); and if I can show that there are additional grounds for supposing that claim to be correct—specifically, for supposing that sympathetic response is *essential* to the experience of at least one kind of expressiveness—then the account that I am offering here will become both more plausible and more (theoretically) respectable. It is to this task that I now turn. I want to suggest that our experience of *human* expressiveness involves, and involves essentially, our capacity for sympathetic response.

We learn about the states of mind of others by coming to understand their behavior, how they express themselves, what they mean by what they do, and how their behavior fits into the rest of their lives. We get, and need, an idea of what it might be like to be them. Their behavior affects us. We see someone sad, and we know that his sadness might harm or upset us; we know something of what his sadness consists in. His sadness fits into our lives, and our responses are part of his. There is, or can be, among people a kind of community of affect, in which we grasp the states of others in the very act of responding to them and learn something of our own states through the responses they inspire. An unfamiliar face, an unaccustomed manner, can confuse our judgment, can show us, through the uncertainty of our responses, that we do not fully understand. Our responses and our judgments go together. When we learn to read a new person we do not simply arrive at a set of more accurate judgments; we learn a set of new responses, and we show and develop in those responses the understanding we have gained. In order to do any of this we need an inner life. A robot might be very good at recognizing expressive signs in a person and behaving in some sense appropriately on the strength of them, but it would not understand what we understand when we respond to a person. For the robot those signs would be precisely like any other signs portending events of a certain kind. A meteorological sign would differ from an expressive sign only inasmuch as the former is discovered and portends events in the sky or in the atmosphere, whereas the latter is found on or issuing from a person's body and promises further events there or nearby. The robot would regard neither as having more than the other anything peculiarly to do with *it*. For us, of course, it is different: we have simply no idea what it would be like to be or to have, except in some dubious and figurative sense, an occluded front; for we don't understand occluded frontedness as we understand sad or angry behavior. Expressiveness, for us, the behavior of others, is an aspect of our world that we can both understand as the robot understands it and can also understand, as the robot cannot, by knowing what it's like; and because we can know what it's like—can feel and *be* the same—our understanding is different from the robot's, and our judgments are richer. The distinction between the understanding available to the robot and the understanding available to us is similar to a distinction that Dewey makes in *Art as Experience* between "recognition" and "perception":

> Bare recognition is satisfied when a proper tag or label is attached, "proper" signifying one that serves a purpose outside the act of recognition—as a salesman identifies wares by a sample. It involves no stir of the organism, no inner commotion. But an act of perception proceeds by waves that extend serially throughout the entire organism. There is, therefore, no such thing in perception as seeing or hearing *plus* emotion. The perceived object or scene is emotionally pervaded throughout. When an aroused emotion does not permeate the material that is perceived or thought of, it is either preliminary or pathological. . . . To perceive, a beholder must *create* his own experience.[14]

In Dewey's terms, then, although a robot might *recognize* expressiveness, only a person could *perceive* expressiveness.

Thus human expressiveness is what it is for us precisely inasmuch as it involves our own affective states; and the perception of expressiveness (and not merely of one kind of sign among others) is conceptually related to our capacity to feel. If I judge someone's behavior to be expressive of, say, melancholy, then I am saying at the same time that I know something of what his melancholy is like, what it would be like to be in the state that his gestures reflect; my judgment is partly felt—which means that in order properly, and in the fullest sense, to attribute expressive predicates to a person, my judgment must

14. John Dewey, *Art as Experience* (New York: Minton, Balch, 1934), pp. 55–56.

always involve an element of feeling, or of affective response. My response is a part of my perception of those qualities. Now of course if those responses are disengaged I may well continue to speak of and to identify (or, in Dewey's terms, to "recognize") expressive qualities around me, but I do so now only like an unusually well warranted robot; my judgments are likely to be schematic and routine, and although with an imaginative affective effort I *could*, as the robot could not, know what it's like, I really treat expressiveness as only one kind of sign among others, probably out of lack of interest, or for convenience. But if my affective responses were never engaged then I wouldn't fully understand the expressive vocabulary I employ—just as blind people can never fully understand the vocabulary of color, though they can use it well; and just as a blind person can have no idea what is the color of an unfamiliar object, so I would be quite unable to make accurate judgments about the expressive qualities of unfamiliar behavior.

One should conclude from these considerations, I suggest, that expressive predicates are likely to be fully applicable in *any* context only if the affective responses are engaged (or if they have been engaged in that context previously). The experience of *human* expressiveness is surely the paradigm case of the experience of expressiveness in general. The ascription of expressive predicates to human beings is surely the primary context within which such ascription occurs. If the ascription of those predicates within that context is fully warranted only when the affective responses are engaged, then, in the absence of reasons to the contrary, it is sensible to suppose that the ascription of such predicates within any *secondary* context—for example, music, or the natural world—is also fully warranted only when the affective responses are engaged (or have been engaged in that context previously). So, for example, although it is possible that someone might have noticed in passing the resemblance between, say, a weeping willow and the posture of a melancholy person, that mere resemblance would never have mattered unless, in contemplating the willow, someone had got some affective sense of what that posture was *like*. It would never have occurred to anyone to describe the willow as expressive of melancholy, or even probably as melancholy at all. Only through the engagement of our affective responses will the contexts in which expressive predicates apply be extended—for example, to the natural world—and our perception of features (like droopy willow boughs) within those contexts as expressive will be coeval with our first responses to them. And as it is with willows, so it is with music.

I believe, then, that the capacity for affective response to music is critical. Melisma would be a possibility without it—rather as some unremarked feature of the natural world might have expressive potential; but until someone has responded to it the possibility must remain unrecognized (or unperceived). I am not claiming that every time we ascribe expressive predicates to musical melisma we do so because we have responded in some way to the music. For, just as in the case of human expressiveness, our responses can be disengaged without altogether incapacitating our faculty of judgment: we can still recognize melismatic features and describe them (elliptically) as expressive; or—if the music has been (responsively) heard before—we can apply predicates in a fully warranted way, on the basis of what we remember to have been the case. But I *am* claiming that unless some or even most of us had responded passionately to musical melisma, music would never have become a context into which the application of expressive predicates had been (even elliptically) extended; and I am claiming that with unfamiliar music, unfamiliar melismatic gestures, passionate response is a crucial part of our coming to perceive those gestures in their full particularity—what those gestures are *like*, what states such gestures might reflect. Thus I think that listeners who love or enjoy music but do not find it especially moving tend to eschew expressive terminology in their descriptions of it, not because melisma is necessarily a mystery to them (they may occasionally experience sympathetic response) but simply because they are more interested in the nonmelismatic aspects of what they hear. The rest of us, although we *can* recognize some melisma purely robotically, as it were, perceive it much more fully and often through our affective responses to it, by coming to grasp its gestures in a kind of felt judgment. To an extent, of course, this is like R. K. Elliott's distinction between experience from within and experience from without, but Elliott does not insist upon the conceptual necessity of the former to the latter.[15] What I have in mind seems altogether closer to Jerrold Levinson's (undeveloped) intuition that "we are saddened in part by perception of a quality in a passage which we construe as sadness, but we in part denominate that quality 'sadness'—or confirm such denomination of it—in virtue of being saddened by the music. . . . Recognizing emotion in music and experiencing emotion from music may not be as separable in principle as one might have liked. If this is so, the suggestion that in aesthetic appreciation of music we simply cognize emotional attributes without feeling anything corresponding to them may be conceptually problematic as well as empirically incredible."[16] A weak arousal theory, then, focused upon sympathetic response, appears central to a full account of the relation between music and the passions; for it provides a bridge from mere *resemblance,* which is what melisma is a form of, to *expressiveness* proper. Melisma is expressive if it's moving.

III

Is this weak arousal theory guilty of the heresy of the separable experience? No. For a sympathetic response—of sadness, say—is related to the music that occasions it as a mode of apprehension of certain qualities *in* the music, as the character of a melismatic gesture is grasped partly in the sadness that it arouses; and

15. R. K. Elliott, "Aesthetic Theory and the Experience of Art," in Harold Osborne, ed., *Aesthetics* (Oxford: Oxford University Press, 1972).

16. Jerrold Levinson, "Music and Negative Emotion," p. 335.

because there is clearly a conceptual relation between the apprehension of something and the thing apprehended, the experience of the former, the sympathetic response, is not an experience which is separable from the experience of the latter, the musical melisma. Therefore the experience of sympathetic response, as I have described it, is ineliminably an experience of the music which occasions it; and it may, if found valuable, contribute to the value of that music.

But this is still to get us no farther in the quest for Mendelssohn's expressive precision. If musical gestures are only related, however, precisely, to passions *formally* characterized, then how are sympathetic apprehensions of those gestures going to render those passions any more precise? How can something expressive of no particular sadness in an infinitely particular way become expressive of an infinitely particular sadness through the sympathetic response it inspires?

To see how, it will perhaps be helpful to return to Ralph, the practice-gesturer. Ralph's behavior is in a sense melismatic—it is expressive of no particular *episode* of feeling, because he lacks the states of mind of which such episodes consist, and indeed (let us suppose) feels nothing, except perhaps a desire to perfect the outward appearances of expression. The precision of his expressive gestures *outstrips* the precision of his affective state, because he either has no affective state, or else, if he does have one, his gestures are not a function of it. So by itself his behavior reveals no precise or particular state of mind. But when we observe his behavior we may gain a variety of impressions. We may not know that his behavior is practice-behavior, and so come erroneously to believe that his gestures do reveal a precise and particular state of mind—*his* state of mind. Or we may be quite aware that his behavior is only pretense and detect in his gestures a semblance of expressive behavior, allowing us to identify (elliptically) only a general kind of state of mind conveyed in an infinitely particular way. Or, in spite of knowing that his behavior is pretense, we may apprehend his gestures partly in a sympathetic response and come to grasp what the corresponding state of mind (which in truth the pretender lacks) is *like*. Thus the expressiveness of his gestures becomes a function not of *his* state of mind, which isn't in the relevant way particular or exact, but rather, on account of the way we grasp or apprehend his gestures, a function of our own state of mind. And that state of mind does have particularity or precision just inasmuch as it is ours, and inasmuch as there is something it is like to be in it. We experience Ralph's gestures as being expressive of the state that, sympathetically, we experience. (Indeed, it should be noticed that the practice-gesturer can also have an effect on his own state of mind. He is an actor, and like any other actor he can, as we say, "get into his part," and come to feel as his character feels. When he does this he is responding sympathetically to his own gestures.)

The state that we experience is an episode of passion. It is not an episode of emotion, for we do not feel what we feel *about* anything: our state lacks a material object. It is instead what I have called a "feeling." In Chapter 1 I described a feeling as a material-objectless state that involves a disposition to experience the world under the description given by the formal object of the co-nominal emotion, so that someone having a feeling is subject to episodes of that emotion. A feeling is also associated with characteristic forms of behavior and with an identifying experiential character (which is what a given feeling is like, and how we know we're having it). When we respond sympathetically to the practice-gesturer the dispositional aspect of the feeling we experience may be more or less marked. It is possible that the dispositional aspect may be so attenuated as to be almost unnoticeable, and this is especially likely if the gestures to which we respond indicate only a general region of the psychological spectrum, however precisely. But it will tend to be the case as well if the gestures are succeeded directly by others of a different character to which we also respond sympathetically: for then a second feeling supplants the first before the dispositional aspect of the first feeling has been realized in any further passionate experience. If, on the other hand, the gesturing to which we respond is of a sustained character, it is possible that we shall come away from the practice-gesturer with our world colored in some way. If the gestures to which we have responded sympathetically are, for example, exultant ones, then we may be disposed, for as long as the feeling lasts, to experience our world and its contents under the description "fantastically welcome," so that we experience episodes of exultant emotion. The practice-gesturer may, in other words, have a relatively lasting effect on our state of mind and cheer us up, or depress us, or whatever. But however marked is the dispositional aspect of our response, it is its experiential character that makes it *this* response and not another; and the experiential character of an affective response can be as precise as you like.

We can see now how Ralph's behavior is not doomed to be expressive, albeit in an infinitely particular way, of passions merely formally characterized. For we may, by sympathetically apprehending his behavior, by entering imaginatively *into* his gestures, experience a precise and particular state to which those gestures correspond. That state will have a cognitive aspect, by virtue of our perception of his gestures as gestures of a certain kind; and also an affective aspect, by virtue of our sympathetic grasp of the state that such gestures reflect. Thus although two sets of similar gestures, if regarded only robotically, may equally convey a general type of psychological state, for example something funereal, in two infinitely particular ways, such gestures may also, if grasped through sympathetic response, convey by their infinite particularity two infinitely particular funereal states—*this* state, and *that*. And it is of these states that we feelingly judge *this* gesture and *that* gesture to be expressive. This, I believe, explains exactly in what way we feel— and judge—the expressive characters of the *marcia funebre* and, for example, the funeral march from Chopin's B-minor Piano Sonata to be so different from one another, and respectively so precise, though both are funereal. And because the states of which we take those works to be expressive are both in fact *our* states, it explains why the experience of music as expressive is often felt to be the most intimate of all aesthetic experiences.[17]

We are now in a position to sketch a reasonably full account of musical expressiveness. Music contains many features that may be heard as melismatic gestures. If these gestures are interpreted robotically, they will be heard to resemble behavior that is expressive of no particular state of mind in an infinitely particular way. The states so conveyed may be described in only a general and elliptical fashion. But these gestures may also be heard as expressive gestures, inasmuch as they are responded to sympathetically. For the perception of melismatic qualities as expressive is not a robotic matter only. Such qualities are in part apprehended in the very act of responding affectively to them. Therefore, to hear music as expressive is to have an experience of the music that has affective aspects, such that the melismatic gestures are heard as being expressive of the state which, sympathetically, we experience. In the responsive listener, such states, because they are a mode of experiencing infinitely particular musical gestures, are themselves infinitely particular; and the states so conveyed, the expressive qualities of the music, may be described in as precise a manner as the nature of those states, and the possibilities of the listener's language, permit. Thus the states of which music is expressive *may* be too precise for words; and because the account of sympathetic response which here underwrites that precision is not guilty of the heresy of the separable experience, such states may, if found valuable, contribute to the value of the music with which they are associated: they may make a piece of music, in Mendelssohn's phrase, "a piece of music which I love."

That's the account that I want to give. But we should ask a

17. See, e.g., Kendall Walton, *Mimesis as Make-Believe* (Cambridge: Harvard University Press, 1989), p. 337.

question: what is there to stop someone from simply *denying* that music is, in my sense, expressive—from saying that the account I have given is simply empty, because there is nothing of the relevant kind that needs to be accounted *for*? At one level, of course, there is nothing to stop someone from saying that. But there is an important reason why no one *ought* to say it. For such a response, if offered as an objection to the account that I have been giving, misses the point of my argument. My argument is not of the form "*If* music is expressive, then my account will explain why that is." If it were, then the envisaged response might make some sense. Rather, the point of my argument is to show how it is possible to account for and defend a number of commonly held beliefs—namely, that music is indeed an expressive art form, that music can be moving, and that music is capable of great expressive precision. A thinker like Hanslick attempts to show that whatever the prima facie plausibility of such beliefs, they cannot withstand close investigation; whereas I have attempted to show that they can. Indeed, I have tried to show how closely those beliefs fit together and how they can be seen to support one another. Thus the only kind of response that's to the point here is one that offers to show that Hanslick is right after all, or at any rate that I am wrong; and it should be obvious that a flat denial of music's expressive capacities will achieve neither of those ends.

IV

The account that I have given is capable of accommodating a number of intuitions apart from Mendelssohn's. Carroll Pratt's remark about music sounding the way that moods feel, for instance, now seems apter than ever.[18] And Roger Scruton's remark that "there may be a sense of 'what it is like.' . . . When I see a gesture from the first person point of view then I do not only see it as an expression; I grasp the completeness of the state

18. Carroll Pratt, *The Meaning of Music* (New York: McGraw-Hill, 1931), p. 203.

of mind that is intimated through it" forms part of a *conclusion* whose tenor I find almost entirely sympathetic.[19] But his way of getting there is quite unsatisfactory, partly because he depends upon the incoherent notions of ineliminable metaphor and irreducible analogy,[20] but most damagingly because he doesn't see the need to say just what permits and what constrains the sensing of "what it is like." For he says nothing of what this sensing involves. It is a strength of the present account that, according to it, both these functions are performed quite explicitly by the concept of musical melisma. Melismatic gestures are the features of a musical work that through sympathetic response are grasped as expressive features; and the expressive attributions made on the basis of sympathetic response are elucidated by appeal back to those melismatic gestures. Thus melisma both permits and constrains our sensing of what musical gestures are "like." It is a matter for music criticism to show that someone who discovers by these means jauntiness, say, or even self-pity in Beethoven's *marcia funebre* has overstepped the relevant constraints (or has fallen victim to a disastrous performance); and such criticism may well be of the kind shown in the analysis by Ferguson discussed in Chapter 5. On Scruton's account, by contrast, it is difficult to know what could possibly count as a descriptive mistake.

A similar difficulty is among those attending a recent suggestion by Kendall Walton. He acknowledges the possibility of melisma but appears reluctant to assign to it any very clearly defined role in either facilitating or constraining expressive attribution. Moreover, the protean account he proposes (though of marginally similar flavor to that proposed here) is obscure in a number of important respects. He says that music calls for "imaginative *introspecting*," and may be

19. Roger Scruton, *The Aesthetic Understanding* (London: Methuen, 1983), pp. 96–99.

20. For a devastating critique of these notions, see Malcolm Budd, "Understanding Music," *Proceedings of the Aristotelian Society* (Supplementary vol., 1985): 239–45.

expressive by virtue of imitating behavioral expressions of feeling. Sometimes this is so, and sometimes a passage imitates or portrays *vocal* expressions of feeling. When it does, listeners probably imagine (not necessarily consciously, and certainly not deliberately) themselves hearing someone's vocal expressions. But in other cases they may, instead, imagine themselves introspecting, being aware of their own feelings. Hearing *sounds* may differ too much from introspecting for us comfortably to imagine of our *hearing the music* that it is an experience of being aware of our states of mind. My suggestion is that we imagine this of our actual introspective awareness of auditory sensations.[21]

So we imagine of "our actual introspective awareness of auditory sensations" that it is "an experience of our states of mind." Thus Walton's listener is apparently 1) aware of auditory sensations (i.e., is hearing the sounds); 2) introspecting this auditory awareness; and 3) imagining himself introspecting his own states of mind. This would be quite an achievement. It is well known that Gilbert Ryle found it hard to believe that someone could simultaneously be in and introspect *any* state of mind,[22] but Walton's listener does this and more. *His* experience has three concurrent objects—the sounds, the awareness of sounds, and certain states of mind; and three separate modes—hearing, introspecting and imaginative introspecting. His listener has, in short, three different experiences at once, only one of which (hearing the sounds) appears to be any kind of experience of the music. It would probably be otiose to ask whether these experiences are separable in a heretical sense, for the degree of psychological virtuosity required to have them all at once would be sufficient to make the number of people to whom the answer might be of interest disappearingly small. But it is worth wondering whether *any* of Walton's experiences actually counts

21. Kendall Walton, "What Is Abstract about the Art of Music?" *Journal of Aesthetics and Art Criticism* (1988): 359.

22. Gilbert Ryle, *The Concept of Mind* (London: Hutchinson, 1949), chapter 6.

strictly as an experience of the music. He speaks of "hearing sounds" and of "auditory sensations," and it is of these that our introspective awareness is imagined to be an experience of introspecting our states of mind. But it is clear that neither the experience of mere sound not the experience of mere auditory sensation (if they are different) is the same as the experience of music; for what is distinctive in the experience of music is the *way* such sounds are heard. And it is certainly not the case that this way consists in becoming introspectively aware of one's auditory sensations. I may presumably, if such introspective awareness is possible, become introspectively aware of any of my auditory sensations—those caused by lawn mowers, for instance; yet this would hardly be to hear the sounds that lawn mowers make as music. But the idea of being introspectively aware of one's own sensations is in any case difficult to make sense of, because it is not clear that there is a difference between being introspectively aware of a sensation and merely having one: sensations are private, and any sensation that isn't experienced privately isn't one. So it seems that Walton's account is not, as it stands, about musical experience at all, but appears instead to be about an improbable way of hearing noises.

We may, however, decide to exercise a certain amount of exegetical license so as to arrive at a happier formulation, which might be phrased thus: we imagine of the hearing of sounds as music that it is the awareness of the nature of our states of mind. Or, to put this in more familiarly Waltonian terms,[23] the experience of hearing sounds as music is make-believedly the experience of being aware of what our states of mind are like. This reformulation has the disadvantage of being rather at odds with what Walton actually says; yet it has the virtues of getting the number of simultaneous experiences down to one, which is where it should be, and of removing all troublesome talk of

23. See, e.g, Walton's "Pictures and Make-Believe," *Philosophical Review* (1973): 283–319; or his "Fearing Fictions," *Journal of Philosophy* (1978): 5–27.

introspection. But it still doesn't make the account more tempting. For what is the reason to think that the experience of hearing sounds as music might ever make-believedly be the experience of being aware of what one's states of mind are like? Walton himself says that "hearing *sounds* may differ too much from introspecting for us comfortably to imagine of our *hearing the music* that it is an experience of being aware of our states of mind." Yet if there is *no* correlation between the two experiences sufficiently intimate for the first, on the face of it, or in some way, to be taken for the second, then Walton's account, even in its most plausible form, falls straight to the ground; for the make-believe mechanism *depends* on there being a correlation of the appropriate kind. Now in the context where Walton's make-believe mechanism has been most widely exploited that correlation is given by the notion of visual or literary representation: the experience of a representation is enough like the experience of the object represented for the first experience to be make-believedly the second. But in the musical case Walton discards the most obvious analogue, for he *contrasts* the kind of experience he's talking about with the experience of hearing music as expressive in virtue of the melismatic gestures it contains. (Actually, even if Walton *had* assigned an appropriate role to melisma, I don't think that his account would have been convincing. For Walton's mechanism would appear to require *rules* for correlating what is real with what is make-believe; and it can be argued that these do not exist even in the experience of fiction—one of the prime domains for the operation of Walton's mechanism.[24] I certainly doubt that they exist in the experience of music.)

So this line of thought seems to peter out, and with it goes Walton's strategy for explaining our experience of expressive music. The account offered here seems much more convincing.

24. See Alex Neill, "Fear, Fiction and Make-Believe," *Journal of Aesthetics and Art Criticism* (1991): 50–52.

It is partly through an affective aspect (which is neither imagined nor make-believe, but real) of the experience of music that the expressiveness of melismatic music is grasped: which is to posit just a single experience. And the sympathetic aspect of that experience is made possible, and is constrained, by the melismatic features of that music. Thus the present account is both more plausible and more economical; and it allows certain kinds of affective response to contribute to the value of the music responded to—which Walton's account, certainly in its original formulation, could never do.

I will end this chapter by showing how the present account can be used to interpret a couple of the rather detailed categories into which the various experiences of music may be grouped. Sometimes a piece of music is accused of being expressive only in a "generalized" way. The imputation is that the expressive musical gesture is not particularly individual, that it is rather all-purpose and, hence, aesthetically unsatisfying. To such a gesture it may be difficult, unrewarding or impossible to respond sympathetically; there may be little sense that there is anything very special about what this gesture is *like.* Thus the failure (of an understanding listener) sympathetically to respond to the gesture, which is a result of the gesture's character, or lack of it, can also signal that lack. The gesturing in the slow movement of Shostakovich's Sixth Symphony seems to me a good example. It sounds as though Shostakovich is simply going through his musical desolation motions again, to gain an effect that is palpably too easily bought, and is far more exasperating than moving; and in a similar but more extreme way, the conventionally melismatic gestures of much film music are also generalized. This type of assessment really claims that a failure of particularity in the music restricts the experience, and hence the description, of the music to the merely robotic, precluding the richness of the felt judgment. As such, it is clearly not to be confounded with an assessment that claims that a piece of music cannot *easily* be described in expressive language.

The first movement of Schubert's "Great" C-major Symphony, D. 944, for instance, is found by Michael Tanner to be of "a very marked individuality," but not "at all readily characterized in emotional terms";[25] and one might say the same of Nielsen's Clarinet Concerto, or of the outer movements of Hindemith's *Mathis der Maler* symphony. Indeed, it is the special achievement of certain composers (Delius and Sibelius leap to mind) to mark out and occupy repeatedly an almost-impossible-to-describe region of the psychological spectrum, a region peculiar to them, without ever writing music that is generalized in the sense mentioned above. Obviously *these* judgments are not derogatory. There is no lack of precision or particularity in the relevant musical gestures (so there is no aesthetic failing), and there is no lack of rewarding sympathetic response. It is just that these gestures connect with states of mind that are more difficult to describe than language, or our use of it, can cope with. And I believe that something of the sort is true of the gestures in many of the musical works we listen to and value the most. Certainly such a sense is conveyed rather clearly in the quotation from Mendelssohn which I have so often invoked; and the capacity of the present account to cover, and indeed to elucidate, cases of this kind should be taken as a partial confirmation of it.

25. Michael Tanner, "Understanding Music," *Proceedings of the Aristotelian Society* (Supplementary vol., 1985): 215–32.

CHAPTER SEVEN

Distressing Music

> The lightning flash of that discovery revealed to me at a stroke the whole heaven of art. . . . But the shock was too great, and it was a long time before I recovered from it. A feeling of intense, overpowering sadness came over me, accompanied by a nervous condition like a sickness, of which only a great writer on physiology could give an adequate idea.
>
> —HECTOR BERLIOZ, *Memoirs*

We have now assembled some of the elements essential to an account of the experience of expressive music, and have discovered reasons to prefer this account to a number of the alternatives. But the present account is itself vulnerable to at least one serious objection, which we must now attempt to address. For if I propose, as I do, to make a form of arousal central to a theory of expressiveness in music, and hence to the *value* of that music, it is necessary to explain how it can be that music expressive of prima facie unpleasant feelings may nevertheless be thought worth listening to, and even valuable, rather than obviously better avoided. This problem—the problem of art and prima facie negative passion—presses quite hard against my account, and also raises difficult questions about the nature of passionate experience. In trying to outline how I believe the problem should be dealt with, then, I hope I can also indicate what a richer, more adequate account of the passions than that which has served us until now might look like.

I

The first thing to notice is that the mere fact that a piece of music is associated in some way with feelings such as desolation or depression does not by itself mean that the experience of listening to it will involve the experience of unpleasant feelings. For the expressiveness of that music may be generalized in the derogatory sense detailed at the end of the preceding chapter, so that its overall character is melismatically apparent without being especially involving. Thus I do not find that the experience of listening to Shostakovich's Sixth Symphony produces in me a feeling of great desolation. I simply identify its melismatically desolate features (e.g., the huge separation in register between strained whining strings and gruff bass support) and, unmoved, I recognize desolation (though no desolation in particular). *These* gestures do not draw me in; they have a staleness about them, a lack of quiddity, which precludes response. On the other hand, of course, I may, in listening to a different work, experience just as little response, but this time through having missed the point. If I merely identify a generalized unhappiness in the finale of Tchaikovsky's Sixth Symphony then the individuality of the gestures it comprises has escaped me, and my failure to respond wretchedly and sympathetically is a sign not of Tchaikovsky's generalized expressiveness but of my own lack of musical sensitivity. Now I think it is clear that music heard like this very likely has little value for the listener—not on account of the types of feeling with which it is associated, for those, unresponded to, are neither here nor there, but precisely because the (experienced) lack of really individual character in the music makes it comparatively uninteresting to listen to at any level. In these cases the problem of music and negative passion simply doesn't arise.

Such cases are to be distinguished sharply from those in which no responses are felt because they have been voluntarily disengaged. By this I do not mean that they have been disengaged by, for example, reading a book or cooking dinner at the same time—*those* listenings are like missing the point of the Tchaikovsky: the particularity of the music's gestures elude the insensitive listener, or the listener whose attention is engaged elsewhere, and the music goes more or less unremarked among the dishes. I mean, instead, a species of listening (to valuable music) in which there is a refusal to be drawn in, so that the particularity of the musical gestures may be relished but remain nonetheless determinedly unreferred by the listener to the realm of expressive experience. In this way I think it is just about possible to gain a "purely musically" rewarding experience of Tchaikovsky's Sixth Symphony without being much moved. But this kind of case certainly does involve the problem of music and negative affect. For it is only if I have a *reason* voluntarily to disengage my responses that I will attempt to do so (suppose I am a listener for whom the experience of music customarily does have a passionate aspect); and the reason in cases of the kind we are talking about seems most likely to be the desire to avoid an unpleasant experience—without, however, having to avoid altogether the music that might be the occasion of that experience. Either I am forewarned (that is, I have heard the music before and know what a passionate experience of it is like); or else I gather what the nature of a new piece is, and cut off in a particular way before I am fully drawn into it.

That this can be done, albeit with some difficulty and at a certain cost, and just *because* music can arouse powerful responses, indicates how misguided is the following line of thought. Music cannot arouse *real* feelings, claims Peter Kivy, for if it did "it would be utterly inexplicable why anyone would willfully submit himself to [some] music. *Tristan and Isolde* is full of music expressive of deep anguish. None, I would think, except the masochists among us, would listen to such music if indeed it were anguish-producing. . . . Peppermints and ice cream are both sold at the Royal Shakespeare, even when *King Lear* is on the bill; for we don't lose our appetites when we perceive the storm of emotions in the play, as we surely would if we *felt* them. (Could Cordelia eat peppermints?)"[1] But clearly

---

1. Peter Kivy, *The Corded Shell* (Princeton: Princeton University Press, 1980), p. 23.

these considerations establish very little. The claim that the music of *Tristan* is genuinely anguish-producing is entirely unaffected by the presence of peppermint-munching, unanguished people at its performance. Some of those people simply don't understand the music, or are uninterested in it, and others are doing their best to listen to it in the way that I have just described—at a slight distance, *because* the music can produce anguish. Still others do not generally have strongly passionate experiences of music, and their experience of *Tristan*, or of the finale of Tchaikovsky's Sixth Symphony, is no exception. Thus the thought that if music produced unpleasant feelings it would be avoided, which it isn't, goes no way toward showing that it cannot produce such feelings. Indeed, some people *will* avoid the music on these grounds (occasionally or always); and in the audience there will also be certain people who have turned up by choice, who understand the music and are interested in it, and who are anguished. Masochists, according to Kivy.

But I doubt that this phenomenon is best to be explained as institutionalized perversion. For it is much more interesting than that—and, indeed, more explicable. It is worth noticing, for instance, that because the sympathetic responses that music arouses are feelings—they are not, in other words, passions *about* anything—they fit into our lives in a less perturbing way than might at first appear. They have, as Jerrold Levinson says, "no *life implications*": "The sadness one may be made to feel by . . . attending to music has no basis in one's extra-musical life, signals no enduring state of negative affect, indicates no problem requiring action, calls forth no persisting pattern of behavior, and in general bodes no ill for one's future."[2] Thus the "masochism" that may be required voluntarily to endure it is not quite the masochism of someone who welcomes a kick in the head. On the strength of this distancing from "life implications," Levinson identifies eight good reasons why an un-

2. Jerrold Levinson, "Music and Negative Emotion," *Pacific Philosophical Quarterly* (1982): 338.

perverted person might seek out and value the negative passion with which music may be associated. These range from the traditionally cathartic to the (expressionistic) thought that sharing unpleasant feelings with a composer through his music will reduce the listener's sense of emotional isolation. Not all of Levinson's reasons are equally compelling, but three in particular are worthy of note: the reward of "understanding feeling," the reward of "emotional assurance" and the reward of "emotional resolution." The first of these involves the greater sense of what a feeling is *like* that the experience of music can yield, as we have the "opportunity to introspectively scrutinize and to ponder the inner affective dimension of an emotion, . . . an improved ability to recognize and to recollectively contemplate this feeling in future. One can deepen or reinforce one's image of what it is to feel melancholy";[3] which fits in well with the account of passionate response urged here, and seems a plausible reason to undergo experiences of the kind in question, even if by itself it does intimate a certain quixotry or self-indulgence in the active seeking-out of such experiences. But it is the other two reasons which are really suggestive. We shall return to the reward of "emotional resolution" at the end of this chapter and concentrate for the moment upon the reward of "emotional assurance." This is the reward accruing from the knowledge, important to a "person's self-respect or sense of dignity," that one has the capacity to feel deeply: "This reward . . . is more naturally associated with negative rather than positive emotions. It is usually not emotions like joy, amusement, or excitement that we have a need of proving ourselves equal to. . . . Having a negative emotional response to music is like giving our emotional engines a "dry run"; we prepare "ourselves for intenser and more focussed reactions to situations in life" and "reassure ourselves in a non-destructive manner of the depth and breadth of our ability to feel."[4] Now I am sure that it is perfectly

3. Ibid., p. 339.
4. Ibid., p. 340.

possible to do this, and that this may partly explain why we think certain prima facie nasty musical experiences are worth having. But I believe that Levinson's assurance relation holds very often in exactly the opposite direction—that it is often the sense that one *does* have the capacity safely to experience certain feelings that provides the assurance necessary for one to go and seek them out (perhaps in music).

II

Let me try to explain why I say this. I can begin best by making the informal observation that the same stimulus may affect people's passions in different ways, and that some of these differences are due to the differing degrees of psychological health or strength enjoyed by the people involved. For example, a person of great psychological resilience is unlikely to find actively pleasant the news that a plane with nobody he knows on board has crashed; but nor is such a person likely to find the news intolerably distressing, or to suffer tearful prostration as a result of it, in the way that a person close to breakdown might. The stronger one is, the better one is able to bear such things; the more "together" one is, the greater is the range of passionate experience that one is able to undergo without undue discomfort. If one is psychologically frail, by contrast, then only a comparatively narrow range of passionate experience is likely to be tolerable. Indeed, beneath a certain threshold of psychological strength, a person may experience even characteristically pleasant emotions as unwelcome, if they are felt too intensely: the very power of the emotion threatens to disrupt an already vulnerable psychology. Hence the hackneyed advice that the neurasthenic, or otherwise mentally friable, should avoid excitement of *any* kind—and not just excitement of a prima facie nasty kind.

These thoughts return us to one of the themes of Chapter 1, where we saw reason to doubt the claim that the hedonic tone of an emotion—the pleasantness or unpleasantness of it—is "dictated by the concept of the emotion," even though most emotions *are* characteristically either pleasant or painful. What it seems as if we ought to be saying instead is that a *tendency* toward pleasantness or unpleasantness is dictated by the concept of most emotions. For what is pleasant and what is painful is not absolute; and it is only a certain way of thinking about emotions which would lead one to suppose that it was. The account of emotion on which we have been relying so far—a version of the so-called cognitive theory—is one that tends, unless one is careful, to divide emotions up rather crudely (into the positive and the negative, among other ways). It does so principally, I think, because the emphasis on belief or thought, on the cognitive component, makes it easy to overlook those other aspects of an emotion which may contribute to the experiential character of an episode of it. Given that beliefs and thoughts can be couched in tidy propositional terms, the temptation is to play down an unruly element that might introduce a strain of messiness into the analysis. Indeed, we have seen Malcolm Budd succumbing to just this temptation in his own theory of emotion. But it is important not to be seduced by the blandishments of epistemologically pristine theorizing. For the emotions are more complicated than an exclusive preference for propositions can capture, and analyses springing from such preferences—which tend to regard emotions as incidental appendages occasionally attaching themselves to the peripheries of the cognizing subject—betray very quickly their discomfort in the face of even the commoner facts of emotional experience.

We need to recognize, I believe, that the pleasantness or unpleasantness of an emotion is often relative, and is only rarely deducible with any certainty from a consideration of the emotion's propositional content (I mention some exceptions to this claim in Section V of this chapter). And if the observations I made a moment ago are accepted, then one of the things to which the pleasantness or unpleasantness of an emotion is relative is the underlying psychological strength of the person whose emotion it is. A related set of reflections appears to have prompted Nietzsche to ask, "Is there a pessimism of *strength?* An intellectual predilection for the hard, gruesome, evil, problematic aspect of existence, prompted by well-being, by overflowing health, by the *fullness* of existence? . . . The sharp-eyed courage that tempts and attempts, that *craves* the frightful as the enemy, the worthy enemy, against whom one can test one's strength?"[5] Indeed, the robust flavor of Nietzsche's questions suggests an analogy that I think is to the point. The kind of psychological resilience to which I have suggested that the pleasantness or unpleasantness of some emotions may be relative is similar in certain respects to physical resilience, to physical fitness. The sensation of muscular strain caused by lifting up a heavy weight certainly *tends* to be painful, but if you are in good physical shape then that sensation can be bracing, enlivening in a way. The rewards of a grueling session in the gym are in fact internally related to the prima facie nastiness of the experiences it comprises. On this model, if I am a person who relishes the challenge of (potentially) negative emotion I may be thought not so much to be giving my "emotional engines" a "dry run" as to be reveling in the resilience of my personality, its capacity to contain and to cope with passionate experiences that *tend* to be painful or disruptive. If this is right, then the rewards I gain are, like the rewards of the gym, internally related to the prima facie nastiness of the experiences involved. In both cases, the experience is probably better described as *grueling* than as painful; and the point at which the gruel becomes pain depends upon how resilient (physically or psychologically) a person is. The important thing to notice here is not the hint of passionate *machismo* that comes across and which the analogy encourages, although that may be real enough, but rather the relation between putting oneself through something, and the bracing sense of satisfaction that comes from knowing, or finding, that one is up to

5. Friedrich Nietzsche, "Attempt at a Self-Criticism," in Walter Kaufmann, trans., *"The Birth of Tragedy" and "The Case of Wagner"* (New York: Vintage, 1967), pp. 17–18.

it. It is this sense, I believe, that helps to explain why certain emotional experiences that might on the face of it seem distressing and well worth avoiding are in fact, by some people and on some occasions, actively sought out—and why they are sometimes sought out in art.

That, essentially is the account I want to give of music and prima facie distressing passion. But clearly it needs to be fleshed out rather; and certain ideas, such as that of psychological "strength" or "resilience," need to be given more content. It is to this mildly labyrinthine task that I now turn.

III

What is it to feel deeply? On a thoroughly propositional account the answer would be likely to be sought in some special relation holding between a person and the proposition which, when believed, is necessary for the occurrence of an episode of the relevant emotion. So, for instance, to feel deeply afraid of one's dentist would be to stand in some special relation to the proposition that one's dentist is dangerous—a relation that goes beyond *merely* believing the proposition to be true. Now according to one neat and tidy account of belief, to believe a proposition is to assent to it, or to be disposed to assent to it. So perhaps when a proposition enters into an episode of deeply felt emotion it is the *degree* of assent that furnishes the depth and that marks off the relation between a deeply feeling person and a proposition from the relation between an ordinarily feeling person and the same proposition. I feel deeply, it might be suggested, when I assent to a certain thought to a particular degree. But a peculiar vigor or consistency of assent does not in fact seem sufficient for or even especially relevant to an episode of deep feeling. "My dentist is immensely dangerous," I think, when I fear him. Do I fear him most deeply, then, whenever the thought of his dangerousness elicits from me the most uncompromising assent? Not necessarily. For I may very well be persuaded that my dentist is, beyond doubt and unquestionably, dangerous and fear him, without my fear of him being *deep,* indeed without my fear of him being automatically any deeper than it would be if I merely suspected or surmised how dangerous he was. It cannot be degree of assent alone that makes for depth of feeling, then.

In fact degree of assent by itself cannot even account for depth of *belief.* I am utterly persuaded, for instance, that Singapore is to the east of Aden and that Beethoven was born in 1770. But it would be odd to describe either of these claims as "deeply held" beliefs of mine. I am merely convinced that they are true; I would assent to both of them with real alacrity, but they don't have the quality that other of my beliefs have—for example, the belief that philosophy is more valuable than ice hockey—which distinguish *those* beliefs as "deeply held." An essential difference appears to be that my deeper beliefs are *evaluative* rather than factual. I would be not merely incredulous, surprised or astounded to find that I had to give them up: I would be reluctant, shaken—even pained. The evaluative nature of a belief is, I suggest, at least necessary for its being deep. But it is not sufficient. Some of my evaluative beliefs are rather casual—for instance, that Respighi's *Pines of Rome* is better than his *Fountains of Rome.* I could give up that belief without astonishment or reluctance, and certainly I could give it up without pain. The fact is that I don't really care about the respective merits of those works, because I don't much care about them individually—I don't think that either of them is very good, and I wouldn't *insist* that *Fountains* was worse, even though I think it is. A casual evaluative belief, then, is unlikely to be deep. So perhaps the requirement that a proposition be both evaluative *and* vigorously (i.e., not merely casually) assented to is sufficient for depth of belief. But this still doesn't get us far enough. For I would assent vigorously to the evaluative claim that steak tastes nicer than crab, without feeling at all tempted to describe this belief as deep.

No. What I think we need is something altogether more like

the distinction invoked by Quine in his discussion of analytic and synthetic judgments.[6] A deep belief, on a quasi-Quinean account, is an evaluative belief that ties into a large number of other beliefs, such that were the belief to be given up it would necessitate the abandonment or modification of all those other beliefs with which it is connected. A casual or shallow belief, by contrast, occupies a position on the periphery of a system of beliefs and is subject to abandonment without causing much, if any, disruption to the system as a whole. This is why it would be not merely surprising to find that one had to give up a deep belief, but also shocking, disorienting and even painful. One has an *investment* in beliefs of this kind; and the degree of one's investment is registered by the quantity of havoc that abandoning them would cause among one's other beliefs (some of which are themselves deep) and by the sheer cognitive inconvenience one would suffer in attempting to reconstitute one's belief system along other lines, incorporating beliefs different from and incompatible with those to which one had grown accustomed. If I were led by some unlikely series of experiences to abandon the belief that philosophy is more valuable than ice hockey, the shock waves that would be sent through the system of my beliefs as a whole would be considerable; and the task of reconstructing a different system would be, to say the least, inconvenient. My investment would have come to nothing; cognitive bankruptcy would threaten, and only a whole new portfolio of beliefs could offer me material for reconstruction.

If this suggestion is right about depth of belief, then it points the way toward an analysis of one way in which an emotion can be deeply felt: a deeply felt emotion is an emotion founded on a deep belief. Thus if one has a deep belief that satanism, say, is a pernicious and dangerous creed, then one's hatred or fear of satanism will be deeply felt emotions. I propose to accept this

6. W. V. O. Quine, "Two Dogmas of Empiricism," in his *From a Logical Point of View* (Cambridge: Harvard University Press, 1960).

analysis and to point out what consequences it has for our inquiry into *negative* emotion. We already know what it will be for a new belief to be painful or unwelcome: it is for that belief to conflict with, contradict or undermine certain of one's preexisting deep beliefs, so that the system of one's beliefs as a whole is disrupted. Thus the person who believes deeply that satanism is pernicious and dangerous will find unwelcome or painful any incontrovertible evidence that the benefits of satanism outweigh its costs, or that most satanists are given to spontaneous acts of generosity. New beliefs that are peripheral to one's belief system, on the other hand, or that mesh in with it neatly and easily, are likely to be greeted with indifference and pleasure, respectively. So, in general, we can say that what the acquisition of new beliefs is pleasant or painful relative to is their propensity for disrupting one's preexisting system(s) of belief.

But clearly this story is going to apply to emotions, too. Specifically, an emotion that involves a belief at odds with one's system of beliefs as a whole is likely to be experienced as painful or unwelcome—as, for example, the experience of an emotion of admiration for a self-sacrificing satanist is likely to be found disagreeable by a staunch opponent of satanism: the cognitive component of the emotion will interfere with his system of beliefs, and he may even reproach himself for his weakness in experiencing admiration in the first place. But we all know, of course, that deeply entrenched beliefs are not quite so easily seen off as this rather analytic sketch might imply. Few of us are so sensitive to contradiction, for instance, or so wedded to the ideals of coherence that we allow evidence which is merely incontrovertible to disrupt our belief systems when that evidence contradicts our deeper convictions. This, indeed, is one of the reasons why most of us have several such systems, not especially compatible with one another, each of which might involve and revolve around a quite separate set of deeply held beliefs (so that, for instance, and to take an extreme case, there are professional evolutionists who manage to devote their spare time to fundamentalist creationism). There are many reasons why a system of belief might prove resilient, and there are strategies both conscious and unconscious for enhancing their imperviousness to revision. For instance one's deepest beliefs might all be true, or at any rate incontrovertible; and provided one recognized this, one would be in possession of an immensely resilient belief system. Or one's deepest beliefs might all be extremely subtle, or hugely amenable to qualification, in which case one's system would again be resilient, and might easily be maintained in the face of apparently unhelpful evidence by rationalization, of both honest and devious kinds. One may be sufficiently oblivious (whether by nature or by design) to the demands of consistency as to be able effortlessly to overlook contradictions between one's beliefs; one may be incredibly complacent and so refuse to take *seriously* any proposition not compatible with one's beliefs; or one may be so stubborn in clinging to one's deeper beliefs that conflicting evidence which cannot immediately be explained away is either forgotten or else hived off somewhere to be defused at a more propitious (or inventive) moment in the future.

So what will be experienced as a negative emotion isn't to be settled quite so easily as I suggested a moment ago. The mere *propensity* of the belief upon which an emotion is founded to disrupt one's preexisting system of beliefs (through its being, as a matter of fact, inconsistent with those beliefs) is not enough to guarantee that the emotion will be experienced as unpleasant. For one's system of beliefs may be resilient in any of the ways just mentioned (and doubtless in other ways, too). Rather, it seems that having such a propensity is one way in which an emotion can *tend* to be unpleasant (that tendency being proportional to the propensity); and then whether it will in fact be experienced as unpleasant depends upon how resilient is the system of beliefs with which the belief component of the emotion comes into conflict. Thus, I want to say, an emotion, when it is in this sense negative, is negative relative to the resilience of the system of beliefs of the person whose emotion it is.

It is not too fanciful to suppose that one's deeply held beliefs, and the wider systems of belief that they structure, are to a degree *constitutive* of one's self, of the core of one's (psychological) being, and so that the resilience of one's system of beliefs— however maintained—is in this sense equivalent to the resilience of one's *self*, at least viewed from a psychological angle. Thus the more resilient one is, the less one is prone to negative emotion. (Remember: there is nothing necessarily admirable about "resilience." It may betoken no more than complacency, stupidity or laziness. Indeed, complete immunity to negative emotion would probably indicate either that one had become ossified, and so incapable of having *any* experiences, or else that one simply had no beliefs worth describing as deep, and so that one's self was resilient only by default.) Now, resilience is a quality that one might relish having and that one might find it rewarding to challenge, through *testing* it against the experience of emotions that involve beliefs of a prima facie disruptive kind, in order to affirm one's capacity either to accommodate such beliefs or else to overcome them (by discounting them, rationalizing them or whatever.) It is in this sense that the voluntary experience of prima facie negative emotion resembles the voluntary experience of prima facie unpleasant physical sensation, as in the analogy mentioned in Section II. The emotion is experienced as grueling rather than distressing, and the sense of "resilience affirmed" that the experience of it provides may be sufficient to encourage someone to seek out that emotion quite deliberately.

IV

But of course he or she cannot seek it out in music. Music, as we have seen, is grasped as expressive through the sympathetic experience of *feelings*, where a feeling is equivalent to an emotion in its formal aspect. Therefore, insofar as the bracing sense of "resilience affirmed" is a characteristic of specifically emotional experience, that sense cannot be derived from, or enjoyed in, the passionate experience of music. But is it true that such a sense is the prerogative of emotional experience alone—that the experience of feelings can never supply it? I think it isn't true; and to see why, it will be helpful to turn in a little more detail to the question of how one's feelings fit into the wider pattern of one's passionate and cognitive experience. What I suggest is that some feelings can be interpreted as *attitudes* of a certain kind, where an attitude is a tendency to regard things in a particular way, often in an evaluative way, which can, when associated with other beliefs and attitudes, exhibit depth and resilience in just the senses detailed above. If this is right, then it will be possible for the passionate experience of music to be negative in the same way that emotional experience can be negative, and for the passionately responsive listener to find bracing or rewarding the experience of music which is expressive of prima facie negative feelings.

It isn't hard to see how this might work. From a person's responses we can gather what sort of person he is, what sort of character or temperament he has, as he shows in his responses what he makes of his world. Perhaps a particular type of passion, such as fear, predominates, so that we come to think of the person as timid; or perhaps the pattern is more subtle, so that although his responses are rather various, and he feels sometimes anger, sometimes chagrin or shame, his emotions seem nonetheless to stem from an underlying timidity, a trait of character that structures his responses without often declaring itself directly. In such a person we discern a dominant, if underlying, quality of affective life, which is quite independent of any *particular* circumstances that may happen to arise for him. And clearly music has the capacity to be expressive of such a quality of affective life. Perhaps the particular passions of which a piece is expressive are all similar to one another; or perhaps they can all be interpreted in the light of some further, unifying state, of which perhaps the music is only intermittently expressive in a direct way. The cheerfulness with which Beethoven's Eighth Symphony is associated, for example, derives as much from a characteristic *tone* in the music, which seems to underlie such diverse expressive states as turmoil, ardor and triumph, as from any direct insistence upon cheerfulness itself. An uncontroversial characterization like this one requires little insight or elucidation. But it does show how certain pieces of music can appropriately be described as expressive of particular, dominant qualities of affective life; and it provides an indication of how other, more sophisticated, critical judgments might be arrived at—as, for example, when Ernst Bloch says of *Elektra* that "a soul is lacking, however lyrical-erotic the prevalent mood. . . . In its deepest passages, Strauss's music wears at best the melancholy expression of a brilliant hollowness."[7] Grasping the robust, cheerful aspect of the Beethoven is fairly easy to do and is distinctly rewarding, whereas the Strauss's "brilliant hollowness" may require the disquieting and rather nastier experience of a more discerning listener if it is to be found out. But in each case the listener comes to know—to feel—the dominant character of a passionate life not his own.

In coming through music to grasp the dominant character of a different affective life we of course experience that character, sympathetically, as a feeling—a feeling that "colors our world," because when we have it we are disposed to experience the world under the description given by the formal object of whichever is the relevant co-nominal emotion. Thus to have a timorous feeling is to be inclined to experience the world as "threatening" and so to undergo episodes of timid emotion, which take as material objects some of the (perhaps genuinely unthreatening) items in the awareness of the person whose feeling it is. It is possible, then, as I suggested in Chapter 1, to describe a feeling as a special and rather all-encompassing kind of emotion, which has the same formal object as its co-nominal, ordinary emotion, but a much more generalized material ob-

7. Ernst Bloch, *Essays on the Philosophy of Music* (Cambridge: Cambridge University Press, 1985), p. 38.

ject—that is, an open-ended set of the present and, if the feeling lasts, future items in a person's awareness: his "world," in other words. A timorous feeling is thus a species of evaluative attitude toward a world that is experienced as threatening.

If the dominant quality of someone's affective life is timidity, he resembles in a number of important and obvious respects a person who more or less permanently has a timorous feeling. He is almost always inclined to experience his world as threatening in some regard and to undergo, on account of this attitude, episodes of frightened emotion (or else, perhaps, of other emotions that depend upon or include this attitude—as a person might get angry or ashamed about a perceived threat). This means that the quality of someone's affective life, if it is distinctive (which is to say deep), is revealing of a distinctive attitude toward the world—of an outlook or, more generally, of a *Weltanschauung*. A person's timorous quality shows that he regards the world as a threatening thing; his cheerful quality, that he regards it as amenable and uplifting. We can impute an outlook to any person in whose affective life we manage to discern some dominant or underlying quality—and an outlook that he himself may be only imperfectly aware of having. Thus, the structural similarity between quality of affective life and feelings (as I have defined them) is sufficient to allow the temporary attitude toward the world inherent in a feeling to be translated into the more lasting and significant attitude toward the world embodied in the dominant quality of a person's affective life.

Music, then, to follow the argument through, can be expressive of *attitudes*. For in coming, through certain pieces of music, to grasp the dominant character of an affective life not our own, we may also become aware of the attitude toward the world embodied in it, as the attitude inherent in the feeling which, sympathetically, we experience.[8] Thus, in grasping the domi-

8. This fact has consequences for musical profundity, which I have tried to explore elsewhere: see "Profundity in Music," in Alex Neill and Aaron Ridley, eds., *Arguing About Art* (New York: McGraw-Hill, 1995).

nant affective character of Beethoven's Eighth Symphony we become aware of what it would be like to have a cheerful outlook on the world, what it would be like to think the world amenable and uplifting; and perhaps, in a more sophisticated kind of listening, we may gather from Strauss's *Elektra* what a brilliantly hollow attitude might be like, and what it would be to look upon a world of highly wrought and glitzy surface. That these factors may constitute part of an understanding of (some) music seems to me to be borne out by reflection upon the experience of listening to (some) music with a real responsiveness, and by the tone of quite a lot of music-critical writing—Michael Tanner, for instance:

> There are some works, of which I take *Tristan* to be, probably, the supreme example, though the *St. Matthew Passion* runs it a close second, if it doesn't equal it, of which it is a prerequisite that one suspends disbelief, not in this or that aspect of the work, nor in the verisimilitude of events in the work, but in the ethos which the work embodies and promulgates. This means that subsequent reflection, in so far as it involves rejection or critique of the work's ethical or metaphysical dimensions, also involves critique of one's reactions to them; but nonetheless it is important that one should have had those dubious feelings and near-beliefs.[9]

Which suggests that we should take seriously the thought that in grasping sympathetically a particular dominant character of affective life, through the experience of a piece of music, we actually come to grasp the attitude toward the world implicit in that character—an attitude which may well conflict with some of our own deeper attitudes.

Thus it is that negative feelings can be treated as negative *emotions* can. Feelings, which we have interpreted as a species of

9. Michael Tanner, "The Total Work of Art," in Peter Burbidge and Richard Sutton, eds., *The Wagner Companion* (London: Faber, 1979), p. 182.

generalized emotion, involve attitudes, which are a species of generalized belief. An attitude, insofar as it structures one's responses or disposes one to see the world in a particular way, can clearly be deep. It can occupy a central position in a cognitive system comprising *both* attitudes and beliefs; and that system can, for any or all of the reasons mentioned in Section III, be resilient. Therefore, inasmuch as the experience of a feeling involves the grasping of whatever attitude is implicit in it, the experience of a feeling will *tend* to be unpleasant to the extent that that attitude is incompatible with one's own, preexisting, deeper attitudes. I think that Colin Radford gets it almost exactly right in his discussion of "being saddened by a great piece of sad music, such as a late Beethoven quartet." He argues that the object of such a feeling can, in the way that I have suggested here, be very general—for instance, it might be "life," or "the human condition"—and he observes that "a capacity to be thus moved by such music is not just a function of musical sensitivity but of capacity, tendency to see life as ultimately sad or tragic. So that a determinedly cheerful person, however musically sensitive, might have little appetite for or a diminished response to, late Beethoven, or might avoid listening to those works entirely."[10] Such feelings will actually be *experienced* as unpleasant, I suggest, to the extent that one's resilience, the resilience of one's system of attitudes and beliefs, is low. A person whose resilience is high, then, may well relish the challenge of experiencing prima facie unpleasant feelings, in order to affirm his resilience by accommodating or overcoming the potentially disruptive attitudes implicit in them. The experience may be grueling, just as the experience of prima facie negative emotion may be grueling. But the bracing sense of satisfaction that comes from knowing, or finding, that one is up to it may be considered worth it, by some people, on some occasions. And

10. Colin Radford, "Muddy Waters," *Journal of Aesthetics and Art Criticism* (1991): 250.

such a sense may motivate one to seek out, or at any rate not to avoid, music which, when responded to sympathetically, involves the experience of the appropriate kinds of troublesome and challenging feeling.

That, then, is a sketch of one way in which the problem of music and prima facie negative passion might be dealt with. But clearly such a sketch covers only those cases where a prima facie negative sympathetic response to a piece of music is *at odds* with the listener's deeper attitudes toward the world. What about the case where the aroused response and the listener's attitudes are perfectly in accord, although both are apparently negative? Well, obviously there isn't going to be any sense of "resilience affirmed" in this. But there may well be a sense of "attitudes affirmed," an essentially agreeable perception that one's own grim view of things is receiving confirmation or support. And again, there will be nothing especially grueling about the experience; nor need there be anything particularly painful or distressing about it. Most likely one's response will have that character of gloomy satisfaction that the misanthrope feels when presented with still more evidence of human perfidy. In the end, then, cases of this kind seem not to throw up anything inconsistent with the account offered here. They appear to raise no new problems.

V

Yet a codicil must be added to all that I have said so far. For the sake of the argument, I have emphasized the structural similarities between emotions and feelings. But these similarities should not be exaggerated. In particular, it should not be thought that *every* emotion can exist in its formal aspect as a feeling; for the beliefs involved in some emotions cannot be generalized into the *attitudes* requisite for the occurrence of any co-nominal feeling. What this means in the present context is that if there are certain emotions which, when they are experienced, are not merely prima facie but *necessarily* unpleasant, then there may not be any feelings which correspond to them; and, therefore, there may be nothing of which a piece of music can be expressive that would make it automatically and for everyone, on grounds of sympathetic response, worth steering clear of.

Clearly this point needs developing. Consider again for a moment the analogy between passionate and physical experience. There are obviously *some* physical experiences that no one could possibly relish, which are necessarily painful rather than grueling. For instance, even the most fanatical pumper of iron is going to avoid getting stabbed or shot if possible. These experiences could never affirm someone's physical resilience, could never underwrite a reveling in fitness—they could only undermine it. And so it is, I believe, with certain emotional experiences. Grief provides a particularly clear example. In Chapter 1 we defined grief as pain at the thought of the loss of a loved one. This means that there is a necessary precondition for the experience of grief—that there be something one loves. But love (which deserves the name) will of course be deep: an indefinitely large number of one's beliefs, attitudes, dispositions and so forth will be enmeshed in a web that has certain evaluative attitudes toward the person loved near its center. Thus the *conviction* that that person is lost must necessarily disrupt or destroy the system centered about those attitudes. There is no question here of a mere *tendency* toward unpleasantness. For insofar as it is true of one that one loved the person lost, and true that one is convinced of the reality of that loss, the room for maneuver (by evasion, accommodation, stubbornness or whatever) which is essential to the notion of resilience is inevitably eliminated. Thus the preconditions for the experience of grief guarantee that grief, if it is experienced, will be unpleasant. To *seek out* grief would be to revel not in the resilience of the self but in its disruption and reduction; and no one who is not a masochist would want to do that. This is not, of course, to say that when one finds oneself in a situation where grief is appropriate one ought to try to avoid grieving: it may well be that one needs to grieve, that it is better for one to grieve. It is only to say that no one sane would voluntarily place himself in such a situation—by, say, deliberately losing something he loves. The case is similar for a number of other emotions. Humiliation, shame and jealousy, for instance, would appear to be logically unenjoyable. To take just one of them: one cannot be humiliated unless one initially has some positive beliefs about oneself, some probably quite deep evaluations of one's own worth; but these evaluations, and the system in which they are implicated, must inevitably be disrupted if one truly becomes *convinced* that one has been shown to be a fool. Room for resilience of maneuver is gone; and the experience of humiliation that results must necessarily be unpleasant. Of course it might be that some people were even so immune to negative emotion. But that would be just because they lacked the relevant antecedent attitudes (e.g., they never loved anything or never esteemed themselves at all), or else because they never became convinced of whatever were the relevant conflicting evaluations (e.g., that the loved one was truly lost, or that they had beyond doubt been made a fool of). What such people would be immune to would be not the unpleasantness of the emotion but the emotion itself. In the absence of either of these disabling conditions, the emotion felt would indeed be grief or humiliation, and the experience would of necessity be nasty.

What the necessarily unpleasant emotions seem to have in common is an element of self-regard. Specifically, the beliefs upon which they are founded refer to some change in one's *own* circumstances, such that the thought of those (highly particular) circumstances and of the relation which (uniquely) they bear to one*self* are essential to the experience of the emotion. Compare this with the experience of other emotions. Pity, for instance, can be founded only on the belief that a highly particular kind of circumstance obtains—that some individual suffers—but without that belief positing any unique relation between those circumstances and oneself. I can feel sorry for the mothers of anonymous disaster victims, for example. It is the absence of any necessary reference to the self in the experience of pity that makes pity only *tend* to be a negative emotion. And because there is no particular self-regarding attitude that one must have as a *precondition* for the experience of pity, there are plenty of ways of responding with pity, but resiliently—that is, without untoward pain—to the suffering of others. So an element of self-regard is necessary to necessarily negative emotion. But now compare pity with still another kind of emotion—take sadness. Sadness can be founded on beliefs that make no reference to the self (as, e.g., when I am sad about the failure of democracy in Indonesia). Thus there is nothing necessarily negative about sadness. But sadness, unlike pity (and certainly unlike grief), can also take an immensely diverse range of things and states of affairs for its object. There is no highly particular kind of circumstance that one needs to believe obtains if one is to experience sadness, which means that sadness, unlike pity or grief, can be *generalized*—that it can be experienced as a feeling, in other words. There is no conceptual difficulty in imagining someone who is sad, but sad about nothing in particular; whereas it is plainly inconceivable that a person could experience pity without believing that *something* suffers, or that a person could experience grief without believing that *something* loved has been lost. (Passions of this latter kind have been described by Julius Moravcsik as "Platonic attitudes";[11] we, of course, have been calling them *emotions.*) It is a criterion of a passion's being a feeling that there be no particular state of affairs which, were a person to become convinced that it did not obtain after all, would at once cancel the passion and make the experience of it not inappropriate, merely, but impossible— which is why music, which cannot represent or convey particu-

---

11. Julius Moravcsik, "Understanding and the Emotions," *Dialectica* (1982): 207–24. See also Peter Kivy, *Music Alone* (Ithaca: Cornell University Press, 1990), chapter 9.

lar states of affairs, can be expressive only of feelings, and why, in turn, the passions of which music may be expressive can never be those passions of which the experience must necessarily be unpleasant: for such passions depend upon beliefs and attitudes which are both highly particular *and* self-regarding, and so which elude the grasp of music altogether.

Thus music can never be expressive of grief, humiliation, shame[12]—or of any other passion that you would need, in principle, to be a masochist in order to seek out and relish in sympathetic response. Which feelings you will *in fact* relish, I have suggested, will depend upon your systems of beliefs and attitudes, and upon how resilient they are; and for some music that will have to be very resilient indeed. To attempt to respond sympathetically and *utterly* fully to some of the music in the first scene of *Tristan's* third act, for instance, would, for most of us, be to court psychological disaster. But on the present account— such extreme cases notwithstanding—it is clear that the *problem* of music and negative passion is to a large extent dissolved. For there is *nothing* that the sympathetic experience of expressive music could involve that might not, in principle, be relished by an un-deranged person. And that, I think, is all that an answer to the problem posed in the first section of this chapter requires. I shall finish with the third of Levinson's "rewards"—the reward of "emotional resolution"—also mentioned in that section; for it will be seen to be at least compatible with the account of music and prima facie negative passion just sketched in—and also to correspond closely with the story about coherently unfolding experiences told in Chapter 3:

> [Passions] presented in and imaginatively experienced through music . . . have a character of inevitability, purposiveness, and finality about them. This is undoubtedly because they seem so intimately connected with the progress of the musical substance

12. Cf. Daniel A. Putman, "Why Instrumental Music Has No Shame," *British Journal of Aesthetics* (1987): 55–61.

itself as to be inseparable from it. . . . [Passion] in a musical composition, because of its construction, so often strikes us as having been resolved, transformed, transfigured. . . . By imaginatively identifying our state with that of the music, we derive from a suitably constructed composition a sense of mastery and control over—or at least accommodation with—[passions] . . . over which we hope to be victorious when and if the time comes.[13]

13. Levinson, "Music and Negative Emotion," p. 341.

CHAPTER EIGHT

Musical Empathies

> It is only if we bestow upon [artists] our soul that they can
> continue to live: it is only *our* blood that constrains them to
> speak to *us*. A truly "historical" rendition would be ghostly
> speech before ghosts.
>
> —FRIEDRICH NIETZSCHE, *Human, All Too Human*

We saw in Chapter 6 that the gap between melismatic resemblance and expressiveness is closed by the sympathetic response of the listener to the melisma that is perceived. The experience of listening to some music with understanding, then, is an experience having passionate aspects, such that certain musical gestures are heard as gestures expressive of the passion that, sympathetically, the listener experiences. Sometimes the passion of which the gesture is expressive will be familiar to the listener from other contexts—from other music, other art, or perhaps from events and experiences in the listener's own life. At other times, and more commonly, only the general type of passion will be familiar, but with shades and nuances different from those discovered in other experiences, so that the listener comes to grasp (as otherwise he or she would not) just *this* particular quality of sadness or just *that* moment of exultation. Such experiences may be very difficult to describe; but the cognitive functioning of our passionate responses can reveal to us, quite concretely, new *possibilities* of feeling or, as, for example, in the *alla danza tedesca* movement of Beethoven's B♭ Quartet, Op. 130—described by J. W. N. Sullivan as expressive of a "gay melancholy"[1]—new *syntheses* of feeling. In Chapter 7, we saw how the experience of music may allow us to grasp certain attitudes implicit in the passions we sympathetically feel. This addition, I believe, enriches our conception of musical expressiveness considerably; and it puts us in a good position to investigate some of the more important of the remaining possibilities inherent in our responses to music. In particular, I hope to show how certain reflections upon *empathetic* response may extend further our understanding of the varieties and complexities of musical experience, and of the value such experiences may have for us. Such an attempt will constitute the greater part of this chapter.

I

The account developed so far can cover some rather complex critical judgments, and in its emphasis upon melismatic expressiveness and sympathetic response it can underwrite many different kinds of psychological characterization (so that the *St. Matthew Passion,* for example, can be described as "religious" not simply by virtue of its subject matter, or of the uses to which it might be put, but because it embodies and conveys a particular attitude toward the world). But it is now reasonable to wonder whether the psychological characterizations thus underwritten—in Chapters 6 and 7—might not in fact be referred to a *person.* We have dealt up to now exclusively with musical expressiveness, so that the passions of which music is expressive have been attributed, if to anyone, only to the listener who experiences them sympathetically. Yet it might plausibly be urged that the passions experienced by the listener are in fact *somebody's* states, perhaps the composer's, and that what really happens is that the listener grasps *empathetically* the passions

1. J. W. N. Sullivan, *Beethoven: His Spiritual Development* (New York: Vintage, 1960), p. 151.

that the music express*es*. Surely Bach was a religious person; so why is not the radiant humility in his music an expression of his, Bach's, own humility? Indeed, the music surely counts as *evidence* of his humility.

We have already encountered a suggestion of this kind in the first section of Chapter 2, and we saw there that "transmission" theories of musical expression tend to fall foul of the heresy of the separable experience. The question that presses here is whether *every* theory of musical expression (as opposed to expressiveness) is bound so to fall foul. Now of course a theory can have shortcomings other than heresy. A very crude expression theory might maintain, for example, that a musical gesture expressive of great misery is one in which a composer has expressed his own great misery, much as anybody else might have pulled a long face; so that his music stands to his misery in exactly the relation that his face might have done. Clearly such an account would be heretical. But its failure to capture an important feature of what we mean when we say that we detect great misery in a work is obvious as well. For a long face is an expression of misery if and only if the person whose face is long is actually miserable. If I say that the length of someone's face expresses misery and then discover that he is not in fact miserable, then I ought to admit that his face did not express his misery. In the musical case, on the other hand, if I have always characterized a gesture as miserable, and it turns out subsequently that the composer was quite content while writing it, I feel no compunction to alter my characterization. The music does not stand to misery as the long face stands to it. The music would still be miserable even if no miserable music had ever been written by a miserable composer; but if no miserable person had ever pulled a long face, then a long face could never have expressed misery. Therefore the crude expression theory misrepresents, and not only heretically, the relation between music and passion. If every expression theory turns out to be like the crude theory, then the search for a nonheretical way of phrasing the theory will be, even if successful, pointless, because the theory will still be false.

In *Beethoven: His Spiritual Development*, J. W. N. Sullivan employs an expression theory that has sometimes, ungenerously, been taken to encapsulate everything that is unsustainable in the crude version. In his book he is, he says, "not primarily concerned" with Beethoven's "amazing constructive power, his dramatic sense, his humour, his impulsiveness, etc. etc.... I am concerned with Beethoven's music solely as a record of his spiritual development"; and, later, that "the function of the kind of music we have been discussing is to communicate valuable spiritual states, and these states testify to the depth of the artist's nature and to the quality of his experience of life."[2] In the often moving main critical body of the book, passages such as this are common: "The man who wrote [the *Hammerklavier*] is already a great solitary. . . . Suffering, it would appear, has harmed him; never again, one would think, can this man melt. . . . The slow movement is the deliberate expression, by a man who knows no reserves, of the cold and immeasurable woe in whose depths, it would seem, nothing that we could call life could endure. It seems as inimical to human existence as the icy heart of some remote mountain lake."[3] Now it is not clear just how apt this description is (the slow movement doesn't seem so inhuman to me); but it would tend to appear that, however apt, the description has been arrived at illicitly. According to Peter Kivy, for instance, "Sullivan explains the expression of music in terms of the evolving state of mind of the composer," so that his descriptions attribute the state expressed to the composer at the time of composition.[4] For Kivy, then, Sullivan's is just a crude

2. Ibid., pp. vii, 36.
3. Ibid., pp. 138–39.
4. Peter Kivy, *The Corded Shell* (Princeton: Princeton University Press, 1980), p. 14.

expression theory, to be rejected because it confuses music with faces and misconstrues the relation between music and passion.

This judgment is probably too harsh, however. On at least one interpretation Sullivan's procedure can be seen to be quite harmless, even if slightly misleadingly set out. For the descriptions he offers are perfectly intelligible, and do not require from us an adherence—even a provisional adherence—to a crude expression theory if we are to find them persuasive or, if wrong (like the mountain lake), at least worth dissenting from. This is because we can read Sullivan's descriptions as elliptical for something like: the slow movement is expressive of a cold and immeasurable woe, icily inimical to human existence, as might be the expression of a person in that state (whom we will call "Beethoven"). We can then agree about the woe, while still wanting to doubt whether the woe of which the music is expressive is really as icy as all that (and accept as we do so the references to "Beethoven" as instances, merely, of a convenient figure of speech—perhaps adopted in order to avoid too passive a mood). This interpretation certainly makes sense of much of what Sullivan says—and so rescues his critical writing, which, since he is a touching and sensitive critic, ought to be pleasing to everybody. But it is clear nevertheless that he means to be taken more literally. Quite apart from the passage already quoted, about music functioning to communicate states that testify to the quality of an artist's experience of life, he also says: "The development and transformation of Beethoven's attitude toward life, the result of certain root-experiences can, I believe, be traced in his music."[5] The "Beethoven" here certainly doesn't sound like a figure of speech.

At this juncture it will be helpful to make some distinctions. The melismatic gestures which I have argued to be the prime source of musical expressiveness are usually quite short (i.e.,

5. Sullivan, *Beethoven*, p. viii.

much shorter than the works in which they appear); and, indeed, most works which *are* melismatic contain many more than just a single melismatic gesture. It is therefore to the melismatic gestures that a crude expression theory ought to assign the (facelike) role of registering a composer's "evolving state of mind," for they are the only places conceivable in which such an evolution might be directly registered in music. Such a theory would, as we have seen, be untenable. But Sullivan, as Kivy doesn't notice, in fact rejects this theory explicitly: the work "of a great artist is not some kind of sumptuous diary," he says.[6] He also rejects a modified and marginally less crude theory. It might be thought, for example, that even if melisma must be a matter of expressiveness only, then the overall *flavor* of a work may still be put down to express*ion*—inasmuch as a composer may express his sadness by writing a piece of music comprising gestures melismatically express*ive* of sadness, so that it is the whole work, and not its constituent gestures, which counts as an express*ion*. Now there doesn't seem to be any very good reason to claim that this can never happen. But if proposed as a general truth (i.e., that sad works, as opposed to sad gestures, always express a composer's sadness) then it is clear that it won't do, and that it won't do for exactly the reasons that the crudest theory wouldn't do. Successive compositions do not reflect successive incidents in a composer's life. As Sullivan says, if someone "describes the A minor Quartet as [expressing] Beethoven's progress from a sick-bed to health we feel that the description is both inadequate and arbitrary. He has failed to do justice to the quality of the experience from which the work sprang, and he has quite arbitrarily invented a cause of the experience. But the critic who should deny any spiritual content whatever to the A minor Quartet, who should fail to see that it could only germinate in the soil of some profound experience,

6. Ibid.

would fail even more signally."[7] This seems to me to be a wholly just remark; though it would probably help to get clearer just what is meant by a work germinating "in the soil of some profound experience," because the recovery from a serious illness, and the suffering from the illness itself, may well be thought to be experiences of a certain profundity, at least potentially. When commentators assert, for instance, that Schoenberg's String Trio, written in the aftermath of a lifesaving injection into the composer's heart, was in part inspired by that traumatic experience, I don't feel especially impelled to doubt it.[8] But perhaps the reason for this (apart from the unimaginable nastiness of the experience, which dramatically outstrips anything to be captured by the term *recovery*) is that the injection is credited with only a partial role in the trio's inspiration, leaving the real "germination" to go on at some deeper level; and perhaps also that the trio has a somewhat neurasthenic feel, wholly absent from Beethoven's quartet, which the makes the contribution of a needle—or at least of an unpleasant physical experience—to its production an immediately persuasive proposition.

Clearly such questions are difficult to sort out. But it ought to be noticed here, in fairness to Sullivan's critics, that Sullivan himself is not entirely immune to the attractions of this style of explanation, whatever he says about the A-minor Quartet. In practice he can seem perfectly willing to correlate events in the life with events in the music, apparently happy to claim that the experience of *these* events (e.g., nephew Carl's suicide attempt) is sufficiently profound to act as a fertilizer, in a way that the experience of a convalescence, as he construes it, is not. But I believe it is possible to make better sense of Sullivan's procedure than this (or at least to suggest what he ought to have been, and

7. Ibid., p. 36.
8. For discussion, see Juliane Ribke's program notes for the LaSalle Quartet's recording of the Trio (1984): Deutsche Grammophon 410 962-1.

perhaps on the whole was, doing); and we will return to the matter in Section III. But for the moment it is sufficient to point out that Sullivan's idea of the "root-experience"—by which a composer's "attitude towards life," expressed in his music, is "largely conditioned"—is a difficult one to handle properly. For it too easily suggests that the experience is a single, concrete experience of a happening that can be dated precisely, rather, perhaps, than some pervasive *quality* of experience, maybe but not necessarily correlated with external circumstance, which is a "root" experience inasmuch as it underlies and conditions a number of the less persistent episodes in a person's affective life (as a feeling or attitude can underlie and condition them). Injudiciously handled, the idea of the root-experience can lead the critic or biographer to put upon certain purported events in the life of an artist constructions that they will not bear, because some new root-experience is needed to account for a departure in an artist's work. And this way circularity beckons: we know that an artist's work expresses spiritual states conditioned by certain root-experiences because we have deduced certain root-experiences from the spiritual states expressed in his work.

II

I distinguished in the previous section between two versions of a crude expression theory—provisionally exonerating Sullivan from the charge of holding either of them—according to the first of which the melismatic gestures in a piece of music register directly a composer's evolving state of mind, and according to the second of which it is the expressive flavor of the work *as a whole* that registers the composer's psychological state. Now it is clearly the second formulation that more nearly captures the spirit of the suggestion raised at the beginning of Section I—that the dominant quality of affective life of which a work is expressive may be attributed to the composer of the work, so that the outlook inherent in the *St. Matthew Passion*, for instance, might be attributed to Bach. But if we are to make anything of this suggestion it will be helpful to take another look at the listener's experience of melismatic gesturing and to consider again the thought, only briefly raised, that any apparent reference to a composer in a (psychological) description of his music should be taken figuratively (to mean, e.g., "Beethoven" rather than Beethoven).

Let us return to Ralph, the practice-gesturer, or actor. As we observe and sympathetically respond to his behavior, we grasp the states of mind of which his gestures are expressive. They are express*ive,* we say, rather than express*ions,* because the states we grasp are states that cannot truly be attributed to Ralph (unless he too responds sympathetically to what he's doing; but then he is in exactly our position). Of course, the temptation to refer to his gestures as express*ions* will be strong, if he is a good actor— and not only because watching him might make us forgetful of our terminology. We may simply be taken in, and erroneously believe that the states of which his gestures are expressive are *his* states. But we might also, and more interestingly, take his ges- tures to be express*ions* if we attribute the states expressed to the character whom Ralph can be seen as representing. Thus under certain circumstances practice-gesturing expressive of exultance can be taken as the expression of an exultant fictional-dramatic character. When it is so taken, it is not because we are in any straightforward way making a perceptual mistake, as a victim of illusion does. Yet nor, I think, is it quite the case that we do something as deliberate as "willingly suspend disbelief," in Coleridge's problematic and useful phrase; and still less that we consciously "perceive in disbelief," which is Roger Scruton's even thornier formulation.[9]

Both these ways of putting it suggest that some rather con- scious decision making is going on, and that an appropriate understanding of dramatic representation is more a matter of

9. Roger Scruton, *The Aesthetic Understanding* (London: Methuen, 1983), p. 131.

the will and its exercise than my experience of drama, at any rate, would have led me to suppose that it was (though I do not deny that in some cases this emphasis might be the right one— when the style is unfamiliar, for example, or the actors inept). It seems closer to the mark to say instead that very often we can hardly *help* but be drawn into the representation, and especially into the representation of the expression of states of mind. And for this I think we can find much of the explanation in the account offered here of sympathetic response. In Chapter 6 I contrasted the "robotic" recognition of expressive gestures, which can result only in the identification of a general type of psychological state, perhaps conveyed in an infinitely particular way, with the consequence of sympathetically *experiencing* a gesture, in which case a state may be grasped in its full particularity as *this* state or *that*. Now, inasmuch as our sympathetic responses involve real instances of the experience of precise psychological states, there is clearly no reason to doubt the reality of those states—after all, they are ours, and there is nothing about them in which it would be reasonable to have any disbelief to suspend. We may even fleetingly see the gestures to which we respond sympathetically as expressions and functions *of* our own states (as Jerrold Levinson suggests may sometimes be the case[10]). But if this would be a clear confusion, it would nonetheless be an explicable one. For when we are presented simultaneously with a real psychological state (ours) and with gestures expressive of that state (the gesturer's gestures), it is not so surprising if occasionally they should seem to be related the wrong way around (or to be related like the chicken and the egg).

Ordinarily, of course, no such confusion arises, and we do not take the gesturer to be expressing what we (independently, antecedently) feel. But what we may very naturally do instead,

10. Jerrold Levinson, "Music and Negative Emotion," *Pacific Philosophical Quarterly* (1982): 341.

as I have suggested, is take the gesturer to be expressing the states felt by a fictional persona whom he can be seen as representing; and this simply constitutes a different strategy for restoring the relation which, in our ordinary experience, holds between the co-presence of a real psychological state and an appropriate expressive gesture. We know that there is a real state—ours—and we know that it derives from "out there"— from the expressive gestures; and therefore, instead of mistakenly thinking that the gestures give expression to our own states, and instead of resting content with expressiveness in the absence of expression, which is unusual in our experience, we construct a persona, "out there," whose states we take the gestures to express, all in a more or less unconscious attempt to save the ordinary appearances. It might be, of course, that this is a very unsophisticated and inflexible thing to do. But it seems certain that it is something we do often; and because a robot— which is incapable of sympathetic response and so could never be presented with a real psychological state as motivation— would not construct such a persona (it would simply take the gesturer for a person showing signs of feeling), it would seem also to be a characteristically human thing to do.

Now what is true of the foregoing, rather artificial, circumstances, will be still more obviously true of any full-blooded case of dramatic representation, where the cues, indeed the incitements, to experience an actor's expressive behavior as the expressions of a constructed persona may be quite irresistible. But in either case it seems reasonable to describe the net effect upon the responsive audience as *empathetic* rather than sympathetic in nature (if not, strictly, in fact), even though the persona to whom the person watching may be said empathetically to respond has been partly constructed, by him, on sympathetic grounds. At the very least, I think, we can say that an empathetic response is often what the response seems like to the person whose response it is; and this response is, certainly at one level, a kind of illusion, or at any rate a largely involuntary experience of something apparent—that is, the state of a persona—as something real. Thus the "willing suspension of disbelief" sometimes held to be the basis of our engagement with fictional characters seems a little strong on the "willing" (unless it just means that we don't mind) and confused on the "disbelief," for it is hard to know what, when we feel that we respond empathetically, we don't believe. The psychological or affective reality of a fictional character is apt to be coeval for us with our first responses to it— initially our sympathetic responses but then, increasingly, as we are drawn or draw ourselves farther into the representation, our empathetic responses.

It is easy to see how these considerations might be applied to some music, and particularly to opera, whose characters are fictional in exactly the way that the characters of any other drama are fictional. In coming sympathetically to grasp the expressive character of a singer's melismatic gestures, or of the relevant orchestral gestures, we may, almost automatically, come to respond empathetically to the persona whom the singer represents. From one point of view the cues or incitements to construct a persona may be fewer than in spoken drama, for opera is often less literally realistic; but because most worthwhile opera so far outstrips spoken drama in terms of expressiveness, any potential loss in involvement incurred by its relative stylization is more than offset by the sheer opportunity for passionate intensity that music affords. In opera, then, we can speak quite properly of musical expression, inasmuch as the melismatic gestures of operatic music may express directly the evolving states of mind of a fictional persona whom we construct and with whom we empathetically respond: Carmen's music expresses her sensuality and, in the final scene, her increasingly desperate defiance. This account obviously differs markedly from the crudest expression theory discussed earlier, and suffers from none of its weaknesses. Because Bizet's Carmen is, for us, ineliminably a persona constructed on the strength of a particular way of experiencing Bizet's music, there is no danger of heresy; and because Bizet's music provides the only possible access to the persona "Carmen," there is no conceivable circumstance in which we could discover that the music is misleading and that Carmen is not sensual after all. Successive musical gestures do reflect (express) successive incidents in the passionate life of an operatic character.

The marginally less crude expression theory, according to which it is not the melismatic gestures that count as expressions so much as the cumulative effect, or underlying flavor, of those gestures throughout a work, can also clearly be reinterpreted harmlessly in light of the present section. For the malevolence that Klingsor's music expresses depends upon none of his musical gestures in particular, but instead is felt irresistibly as a result of them all; and the claim that the malevolence expressed is Klingsor's is neither heretical, nor subject to revision as a result of *any* extramusical evidence, for the persona "Klingsor" is ineliminably founded upon the experience of Wagner's music.

But it should be apparent from the emphasis given above to the practice-gesturer that musical express*ion,* in the senses given by the previous two paragraphs, is not a prerogative of opera alone, even if in *these* senses it is the prerogative of music where experience may involve the listener's constructing a fictional persona. Song can clearly involve the expression of passions in both ways: Delius's *Sea Drift,* for instance. At the (melismatic gestures accompanying the) words "and I singing uselessly, use-lessly" the "sea-bird" persona is heard as expressing a passionate sense of loss; and yet the affective character expressed by the whole is the sea-bird's own underlying quality, a strangely *affir-mative* quality of regret. With purely instrumental music the matter is rather more difficult, and I suspect that it is impossible to give any secure indication of which kinds of instrumental music support or invite the construction of an express*ing* persona by the responsive listener. But that some purely instrumental works *do* support or invite this seems certain. For example, I find it very difficult to conceive of an experience of

Mahler's Ninth Symphony which does not involve hearing it as, inter alia, the expression of the evolving psychological state of a highly distinctive persona—as a kind of soul journey, in other words. Nor can I easily imagine what it would be like not to hear in Chopin's G-minor Ballade, as a whole, the expression of a persona of almost overardent sensibility, though not of a persona whose condition evolves a great deal as the piece progresses. Most of Ravel's music, on the other hand—to choose just one from any number of possible examples—suggests to me no persona whatever, so that my experience of his music (which I admire and enjoy: there is no direct question of *value* here) only rarely involves charting the progress in, or grasping an overall character of, empathetically experienced expres*sion*. (Maybe the Piano Trio is an exception.)

It might perhaps be possible to formulate a rule of thumb—not for deciding which pieces of music invite the construction of a persona, but for deciding which kinds of music are more likely to invite the construction of one type of persona than of the other: which sort of music might invite an evolving persona, and which sort an overall, static persona. The question hinges on the contrast between a developing narrative and a character study (although of course the two are not mutually exclusive); upon the predominance or otherwise of musical *drama*, in other words. As the Classical sonata style superseded the Baroque, the "dramatic" (in Tovey's words) superseded the "architectural": "the mere rendering of sentiment was not dramatic enough; . . . [it] was replaced by dramatic action. . . . [Bach's] seamless, almost uniform flow, . . . in Haydn becomes a series of articulated events—at times even surprising and shockingly dramatic events."[11] Or, in Joseph Kerman's words,

> Passages in rest alternate with passages of impulse; yet they do not simply alternate in the older fashion, but rather grow in and

11. Charles Rosen, *The Classical Style* (London: Faber, 1971), p. 43.

out of one another in a way that gives a vital impression of leading and arrival. . . . Moreover, the new dramatic style made it possible to join together elements in essential contrast—soon treated as elements in essential conflict: abrupt changes of feeling were at first juxtaposed, then justified and developed until a final resolution lay at hand. Music in a word became psychologically complex. . . . We may compare [the sense of progress in Beethoven's C♯ minor Quartet, Op. 131] to a progress in Hogarth's sense; in these terms, the five movements of the *First Brandenburg Concerto* show only the general unity of a well-planned room in a picture gallery.[12]

Thus the dramatic sonata style, with its newfound "psychological complexity," was able to present a developing passionate narrative, so that it could "reveal the *quality* of action, and thus determine dramatic form in the most serious sense."[13]

Now of course it would be foolish to claim on these grounds that all music after Haydn invites the listener to construct an evolving persona of whose states the music is heard as an expression, because much of it seems not to; and only in the face of dozens of counterexamples (for instance, Monteverdi's *L'Incoronazione di Poppea*) could it be maintained that no music does this *before* Haydn. But the presence of dramatic development does at least seem to be necessary if the listener is to gain the impression that a "soul journey" is being expressed; and the absence of such development must equally ensure that only a character-study persona, if any, can be constructed (though it should be emphasized again that this doesn't mean that the music is any the *worse* for this). It is instructive to notice that the complete abolition in much contemporary popular music of rhythmic or harmonic interest—crucial factors in the dramatic qualities of the music of the last two centuries—has resulted almost immediately in (although it probably also springs from)

12. Joseph Kerman, *Opera as Drama,* rev. ed. (London: Faber, 1989), p. 59.
13. Ibid., p. 9.

a drastic reduction in psychological complexity; so that in terms of this discussion, to paraphrase Kerman, the successive sections of many songs show only the general unity of a disgruntled queue at a bus stop. And this is a disaster when the music, unlike Baroque music, has nothing *else* of interest to offer.

It is a matter for musical criticism—that is, for sensitive listening—to decide whether the construction of an expressing persona is appropriate to a particular piece of music or not; but the foregoing considerations should offer at least some indication of whether that persona is likely to be an evolving one. The important thing to remark here, however, is that the overall effect of following the progress of an evolving persona in dramatic music may well be the construction of a character-study persona similar to that invited by certain nondramatic pieces of music. The reason for this is precisely the reason offered in the previous chapter why we can discern, amid diversely expressive melismatic gestures, an underlying and dominant quality of affective life, a characteristic attitude. The soul who journeys through Tchaikovsky's Sixth Symphony, for instance, is clearly a depressive who loves and despairs of his world in equal measure; and the sad strength of Delius's sea-bird glows through all the dashed hopes and desolation of his passage. A state of soul, then, can be expressed in music—the state of a persona constructed in the musical experience of a responsive listener. Which is why "much expressive music is heard as containing states of mind that create the impression of a personality whose depth or shallowness of feeling, vitality or torpor, sincerity or insincerity, warmth or coldness attracts or repels. And the fact that our ordinary human sympathies and antipathies are engaged by expressive music is dependent not merely upon our being made aware of a state of mind by the music, but on our entering imaginatively into that state of mind."[14] And, of course,

14. Malcolm Budd, *Music and the Emotions* (London: Routledge and Kegan Paul, 1985), p. 149.

if the states of mind expressed by the music and responded to by the listener are deep and distinctive, or if, in several works by the same composer, they are similar or closely related, then we are apt to think of the persona whose states these are (or of the superpersona, if several works are involved) as the composer, or the "composer."[15] And if a superpersona's state develops in successive works then we are apt to think of the music as an expression of its "composer's" spiritual development.[16]

III

Do we need the scare-quotes? Are we obliged to regard the Beethoven whose progress through his works is charted by Sullivan as only "Beethoven," as only an extraordinarily interesting superpersona? Or can we get to know the real Beethoven? A full answer to these questions would take us far afield, of course, into a probably unprofitable discussion of the intentional fallacy, and of the many advantages to be secured by committing it. So I propose to confine myself here to a few common-sense remarks. "In his greatest music," writes Sullivan, "Beethoven was primarily concerned to express his personal vision of life. This vision was, of course, the product of his character and experience. Beethoven the man and Beethoven the artist are not two unconnected entities, and the known history of the man may be used to throw light on the character of his music."[17] This sounds very reasonable, but of course it has the dubiousness which comes through suspected association with the crude expression theories dismissed in Section I, and I have already pointed out one of the dangers, not always avoided by Sullivan, in his related technique of the "root-experience" (although it should be said that because Sullivan, as every

15. For more on the persona-as-artist see Jenefer Robinson, "Style and Personality in the Literary Work," *Philosophical Review* (1985): 227–47; and Bruce Vermazen, "Expression as Expression," *Pacific Philosophical Quarterly* (1986): 196–224.
16. Cf. R. K. Elliott, "Aesthetic Theory and the Experience of Art," in Harold Osborne, ed., *Aesthetics* (Oxford: Oxford University Press, 1972), p. 157.
17. Sullivan, *Beethoven*, pp. vii–viii.

artist's biographer ought to be, is much more interested in the art than in the life, it is the account of the life that suffers when he goes astray and starts explaining things in circles, and not that of the art; which is to say that nothing calamitous happens). Nevertheless, the passage itself does not blatantly contain signs of such shortcomings and so should be taken seriously.

It is clear that the "personal vision of life," the product of "character and experience" to which Sullivan refers must, if it is to be expressible in music, be the same thing as the "outlook" or "attitude" inherent in a quality of affective life that I discussed in Chapter 7. We may note here that such an attitude might in its essentials be indistinguishable between very different characters, if their circumstances (or experiences) are appropriately different as well; and we can see that it will be necessary already to know about two of the three terms (outlook, character, circumstance) if we wish to discover anything about the third. If someone's circumstances have been odious in the extreme and yet he evinces a forbearing and trustful attitude toward the world, we can deduce of his character that it is either saintly or extremely foolish. Similarly, from a saintly character in odious circumstances we would expect forbearance, and from the same character with the relevant attitude we would infer something in his circumstances that needed to be forborne—that is, something odious. But none of these elements by itself is sufficient to establish much about either of the others.

Sullivan claims that "the known history of the man may be used to throw light on the character of his music." We can now see that this claim is false, at least if taken at face value. For if by "known history" is meant a man's circumstances, or experiences, and by the "character of his music" is meant the "personal vision" or attitude toward the world expressed in his music, then, as we have just seen, the former is insufficient to tell us about, or "to throw light on," the latter—which is why the much-trumpeted fact that Shostakovich lived under Stalinism is such a peculiarly unrewarding thing to know if one is trying to grasp what his music is like (though of course it might be useful to know this sort of thing if one is curious about *why* the music is like that—the demands of Soviet optimism, etc.; but knowing such facts can be of no help in getting at the *what* of the music). Sullivan's claim is false, in the first place, because you need to know two of the three elements if you are to deduce the nature of the remaining one; and false, also, because the quality of the music that a composer's history is supposed to illuminate can be grasped *only* through an experience of the music itself; and therefore no other kind of appeal—for example an appeal to the composer's character or circumstances—carries the least weight, *unless* one espouses a crude expression theory.

This second consideration is clearly powerful enough to render pointless any attempt to reinterpret "known history" so that it includes both circumstances *and* character (which might have been suggested in order to bypass the first consideration), for the evidence of the music simply *isn't* to be corroborated, or undermined, from any other quarter. In fact, what we can now see is that the only deductive use that the circumstance/character/outlook arrangement could possibly serve would be to provide pointers toward the *life*—probably the character, assuming we knew the works and the history (although even so the pointers would have to be tentative ones: the three-way arrangement we've been using is *very* schematic). And this, I think, is what Sullivan actually does with it, as distinct from what he says he does with it. Inasmuch as he is a biographer, he uses the music to throw light on the life (which must be right: would any evidence for, say, Tchaikovsky's desperately depressive character be complete without reference to his music?—and does not the *St. Matthew Passion* music *clearly* show Bach's humility?); while as a critic he gives overwhelming pride of place to the music. To be sure, he does speak of the music as if it were the direct expression of the man Beethoven's "vision of life." But he is sufficiently faithful to the spirit of the music always to prefer the evidence of "Beethoven" the superpersona, where the two conflict, so that it is the man who is misrepresented (as when Sullivan trips over his "root-experiences"), while the music comes through, perhaps in mildly figurative garb, quite unscathed. His spiritual biography is therefore most signally, and entirely properly, a biography of "Beethoven."

So I tend to think that we do need the scare-quotes, at least technically. But there are a number of things that don't follow from this. For example, it certainly does not follow that Sullivan is wrong when he says of the A-minor Quartet that it would be a failure not to see that the work could only have germinated "in the soil of some profound experience"; for surely he is right. But this, of course, is simply a case of using the music to illuminate the life. For the man who wrote the music containing *that* persona cannot but have had an extraordinarily rich quality of experience, although a quality of experience that can only securely be indicated by saying that it was such that he could write the A-minor Quartet. We make a mistake only when we take that quality to be necessarily the same as the one expressed by the music's persona.

The deductive traffic must always flow from the music to the life, then. The fact that Wagner was able to make those strong and nobly diatonic motifs arise naturally even from the densely chromatic textures of *Parsifal*, for instance, apart from representing an astonishing technical achievement, which it certainly does, also bears incontrovertible witness to the *musical* depth of his psychological insight. Not all the biographical evidence in the world could have established just that quality in him, as may be seen by comparing Strauss's efforts in the same direction— for example, the way the portentous Jokanaan motif arises from the equally chromatic textures of *Salome*. If, as seems hard to believe, Strauss *was* in life a man of great psychological insight, then the banality of that effect betrays his shallower musical side (and I'm not speaking of a *technical* failure here: only a superb technician could have given himself away so thoroughly). Wagner's psychological insight, then, and Strauss's comparative lack of it are not *expressed* in their music but instead make their music possible, and so can be inferred back from it. No one, we want to say, could have done *that,* unless he had *these* qualities: but "these" are not qualities of the music. The qualities of the music, and of the persona whose construction the music invites, can be grasped only through the experience of that music by the responsive listener.

So what I suggest is this. The experience of listening to some expressive music can be described as the experience of coming to grasp or understand the state of mind of a persona whom we construct as we listen to the music and sympathetically respond; but with whom it will be reasonable to say, inasmuch as we refer that state elsewhere, to the persona that we hear *in* the music, that we in fact empathetically respond. When our experience of music is of this kind, we hear express*ive* music as music which express*es* a state of mind that is not ours—although we come to know what that state is like—but the persona's; and the outlook on the world, or the attitude toward it, inherent in that state of mind, we hear as expressed in the music *by* the persona. The experience of expression in music, then, is a possibility for the listener who experiences certain pieces of music in a highly particular way.

Conclusion

At the heart of the connection between music and the passions lies the melismatic gesture, which resembles items in the expressive repertoire of extramusical human behavior, either physical or vocal (although it should be said that in a highly musical culture some of *that* behavior is quite likely to derive *from* music, so that there might be an element of give and take; but this possibility does not affect the basic point). If one is to hear a melismatic gesture as a musical gesture of any kind, one's experience must possess certain properties, so that one is capable of hearing sounds in a certain way. If one can do this, one understands music, at least in a rudimentary sense. It is possible that one will hear qualities, in such gestures as are melismatic gestures, that lead one to characterize the music in certain broad psychological terms. But the inclination to do this, and the capacity to grasp the *precise* quality of the gestures one hears, will be slight or absent if one's experience does not also involve a certain kind of response—a sympathetic response. One can, as an understanding listener who responds sympathetically to the melismatic gestures of expressive music, grasp, in a kind of felt judgment, the precise passion of which those gestures are expressive. The gestures are expressive of the passion which, sympathetically, one experiences. In addition, the passions one grasps may be heard as the expressions of a persona whose gestures those are, but whom one in fact constructs as one responsively experiences the music; and one may respond empathetically, as one does this, to the outlook or attitude toward the world that is inherent in the passions or states of mind now attributed to the persona.

I hope that I have made it clear throughout that I do not want to claim exhaustiveness for this account. It is quite conceivable that other, perhaps many other, elements in a musical work may have expressive capacities and that these, once identified, will have to be explained by a method different from that employed here. Equally, someone might produce a story that shows how music, perhaps on the strength of those other currently unidentified expressive elements, can express states of mind in a more literal way than is allowed for by my style of explanation. But what can be said for the present account is that it does chart *one* route through the theoretical minefield that separates music from significant states of mind (a separation that is not apparent in the musical experience of most listeners), and that by doing so, it does permit many of the descriptions offered by listeners as descriptions of their musical experience to be interpreted and explained. If this account has a great deal less to say about musical express*ion* than it does about express*iveness*, perhaps surprisingly, then I trust that the reasons are now clear—not least the reason that expressiveness, being a condition of expression, must take theoretical priority if the question of expression is usefully to be raised at all. (In any case, the hard distinction between the two terms is largely a technical matter: it is not the listener trying to describe his or her musical experience who needs devotedly to bear the distinction in mind, only the philosopher who tries to describe the listener trying to do this.) In establishing a passionate basis for one species of musical experience, then, this account manages to make sense of that experience and of our characterizations of it. Sometimes, indeed, being not at all monolithic, the account manages to make several senses of that experience, which must certainly count as a strength when one remembers just how diverse it is possible for musical experiences to be.

Thus the full story given above may well not fit the experience of many pieces of music. But there are plenty of stopping-off points. Some music may not be expressive at all (in which case the story need hardly be started); some music which does have expressive features may have few or no features that hold the attention principally by virtue of their expressiveness (e.g., Scarlatti in Chapter 5); some music may be full of melismatic gestures, but not gestures sufficiently individual to invite the listener's imaginative response (e.g., Shostakovich in Chapter 6); and some music may reveal itself, through the sympathetic responses of the listener, in its full expressive particularity without, however, inviting the construction of a persona (e.g., Ravel in Chapter 8). Music, and the experience of it, is of course tremendously various; and it is usually no criticism of a work to say that it stops off from the story very early. But I do believe that much of the most valuable music we have goes all the way.

The account I have given of our musical experience has been vetted at every point for heresy. So if there is anything valuable in the experience of coming to understand the passions or the states of mind of a constructed persona, then there is ample and legitimate cause for valuing the music which uniquely occasions that experience. I have already quoted J. W. N. Sullivan's remark that the valuable spiritual states contained in Beethoven's music "testify to the depth of the artist's nature and to the quality of his experience of life."[1] Of course Sullivan really means those spiritual states to *be* that deep nature and that quality of experience, so that it is *these* which are contained in the music. But then, as

1. J. W. N. Sullivan, *Beethoven: His Spiritual Development* (New York: Vintage, 1960), p. 36.

we saw in the previous chapter, he cannot also hold those states to be Beethoven's. The solution, obviously, is to put scare-quotes around the artist, forget about Beethoven, and say that the experience of his music involves the construction of a persona whose depth of nature and other qualities are exceptional, so that the music is valuable, among other reasons, because the experience of (an encounter with) states of this exceptional kind is itself valuable and is, necessarily, *only* to be had in the experience of that music. And put like that, I believe it. It is hard to see how the opportunity to grasp, or to gain at least an inkling of, a state of soul or an outlook of extraordinary depth could fail to be valuable to us. The intensity of the musical experience and the quality revealed in it may themselves be pleasurable, and valued for that. But inasmuch as the experience is very intense, and the state revealed is felt to be of the greatest significance, it may be valued *in spite of* any prima facie unpleasant qualities it may have. Indeed, because the state whose significance we feel can be revealed to us only through our own responsive constructions, we must ourselves be responsible in part for whatever wounds we receive. As Nietzsche says (with my scare-quotes) "It is only if we bestow upon ['artists'] our soul that they can continue to live: it is only *our* blood that constrains 'them' to speak to *us*"[2]—and we would never bestow these things unless we wanted to know what "they" had to say.

But to conclude, as seems appropriate, with a final remark from Sullivan: musical revelations, he says, "have a strangely haunting quality. We may be unable to earn for ourselves the capacity to utter the prayer of thanksgiving of the A minor Quartet, or to reach the state of final serenity of the fugue of the C-sharp minor Quartet, but we can henceforth take but little

2. Friedrich Nietzsche, *Human, All Too Human* (Cambridge: Cambridge University Press, 1986), 2:126.

account of attitudes towards life that leave no room for these experiences, attitudes which deny them or explain them away."[3] The desire to expand and to refine the quality of our experience in the musical encounter with exceptional states of mind—*that* is why much of the music we think most expressive, most informed by passion, is included among the music we value most highly. Music, value and the passions go together; and in trying to trace and to account for some of the connections between them, I hope in this book to have shown at least one reason why that is.

3. Sullivan, *Beethoven*, pp. 173–74.

Index